THE JUNIOR LEAGUE OF NORMAN CULINARY COLLECTION

Simply Good Taste

ISBN 978-0-9854785-0-6 (Belmar Cover)
ISBN 978-0-9854785-1-3 (Modern Environment Cover)
ISBN 978-0-9854785-2-0 (Dillard Cover)

For additional copies, please contact:
Junior League of Norman
c/o Cookbook Committee
300 W. Gray Street, Suite 104
Norman, OK 73069
(405) 329-9617
www.JuniorLeagueofNorman.org

Photo Credits:
Megn Sparkman: Cover, 6, 9, 20, 25, 28, 36, 39, 46, 50, 56, 68, 73, 83, 85, 86, 90, 104, 106, 108, 111,
  112, 116, 119, 134, 137, 141, 142, 150, 158, 169, 171, 181, 184, 190, 193, 194, 195, 199
Becca Vermelis: Welcome to Norman, 3, 11, 12, 19, 27, 49, 55, 67, 94, 101, 102, 123, 124, 147, 148, 183, 216, 223
Valorie Wakefield: 1, 10, 13, 14, 17, 93, 131, 132, 157, 207, 210, 215, 219, 221
Nonna's: 187
Legends': 71
Jolene Curry: 39, 40

A Taste of Sooner Heritage

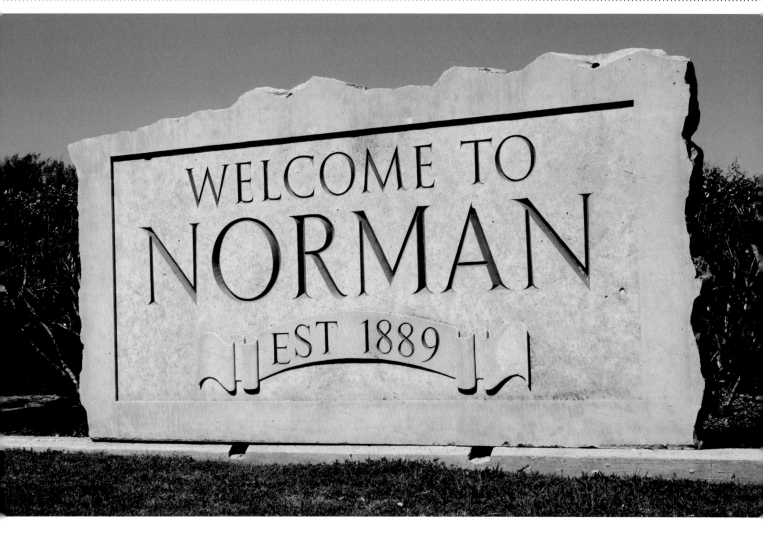

Norman has a rich and unique history that began in 1889 with the Oklahoma Land Run. An estimated 150 people, many in covered wagons known as "prairie schooners," settled along the banks of the Canadian River, and the town of Norman was born.

One year later, our citizens donated 40 acres of land for a campus site, and founded the University of Oklahoma, which enrolled 100 students in 1895. Today, Norman has more than 110,000 residents, and the University of Oklahoma has approximately 30,000 students enrolled.

The nickname, "Sooners," was originally associated with settlers who headed west before the official beginning of the Land Run on April 22, 1889. It has now come to symbolize the spirit of progressivism that characterizes our community. Sooners are energetic, "can-do" individuals, who take pride in pioneering new developments. Much of our areas developed can be credited to the cattle and oil industries, but we have also become known for our prosperous wheat, pecan, and peach farms.

Norman is a town full of tradition, and its citizens are known for their genuine warmth and friendliness, as well as for their diverse cultures. It has a wide selection of quality restaurants, many of which have contributed to this cookbook. The variety ranges from the southwest favorites of a pioneer cook, to the cosmopolitan flair of a university town. We hope you enjoy a "taste" of Sooner fare.

Contents

A History

The Junior League of Norman is an organization of women committed to promoting voluntarism, developing the potential of women and improving the community through the effective action and leadership of trained volunteers. Its purpose is exclusively educational and charitable.

The Junior Service League of Norman was incorporated in 1975. In 1983, the League was voted into the Association of Junior Leagues as the 252nd League. The first project was Reading Is Fundamental, which continued well into the 2000's.

During the 1980's, the following programs were created:
· Parents Night Out for the Handicapped
· Stovall Museum Outreach Program
· Funding of a birthing room at Norman Regional Hospital
· Early Rider
     (an infant car seat loan and education program)
· Boomer Bargains
· Preschool Vision Screening
· The Chemical People Project
· Volunteer of the Year Awards
     (with the United Way of Norman)
· We Help Ourselves
     (a personal safety program for kids)
· Kids On The Block
     (disability awareness program for elementary children)
· Health For Friends
· The Parenting Project
· Just Like New Thrift Shop
· The Sooner Sampler Cookbook
· Targeted Intervention Program
     (after school program for at-risk students)
· Domestic Violence Seminar
· Forum on Teenage Parenting
· Parents As Teachers Program

Some of these programs were handed off to other agencies and some created their own governing bodies as their size increased.

During the 1990's, the League embarked on the following:
· Better Babies
· Elderly Day Out
· Fall Festival
· Baby Steps
· Expansion of Reading Is Fundamental to the
     homeless shelters
· Preventing Shaken Baby syndrome
· Assist the Sam Noble Oklahoma Museum of
     Natural History
· Teen Volunteer

The League has also developed position statements on volunteerism, adoption, and child safety and partnered with numerous agencies to bolster our efforts.

During the 2000's, the League:
· Assisted with Neighborhood Centers
· Revised and reprinted the *Sooner Sampler* Cookbook
· Made Baby Steps our signature project
· Implemented Kids in the Kitchen program for nutrition
     and healthy choices
· Established the Monster Dash 5K Run/Family Fitness Event
· Partnered with the Regional Food Bank to provide back
     packs of food for secondary school students
· In 2012, a 25th anniversary tribute to the *Sooner Sampler*
     cookbook was published

The Junior League of Norman has made a tremendous impact on the community as evidenced by the many programs that still stand today. The women who started this organization and the women who continue the good work today are passionate about building a better community.

Junior League of Norman Projects

The Junior League of Norman is committed to voluntarism and community service. This commitment is evident through our trained members who give their time to Junior League projects.

Our projects are designed to provide maximum benefit to our community through our League volunteers, community partnerships and direct financial support. Each Junior League of Norman project reinforces our League's mission, as well as our commitment to our focus of fitness and nutrition.

Baby Steps Baby Steps helps teen parents complete their high school education so they can reach their goals, become productive citizens, and effective, nurturing parents. Baby Steps is a coalition between the Junior League of Norman, Norman Public Schools, Crossroads Youth and Family Services, and the Center for Children and Families. The Junior League of Norman opened Baby Steps in 1993. More than 130 pregnant and parenting teens have graduated high school while participating in the Baby Steps program.

Baby Steps is an Early Head Start program. It is accessible and free. Teen parents can complete their high school education while their children receive quality early childhood education services. Baby Steps enhances parenting skills by providing daily childcare classes and hands-on lessons with the children in the center. Preventing child abuse, neglect, and negative parenting are high priorities.

Baby Steps continues its positive influence on these students and their children, in part, through the support of many generous donors.

Done In A Day Through the "Done in a Day" (DIAD) program, the Junior League of Norman is able to provide assistance to other non-profit agencies in the community with short-term volunteer needs. Various 501 (c) (3) organizations are invited to submit applications to JLN to be considered as a DIAD project for the current year.

JLN is not only able to offer volunteers to complete a project, but limited funding is also available.

Food for Kids One in five children in Oklahoma is likely to be hungry every day, according to the Regional Food Bank of Oklahoma. For many children, hunger isn't just an occasional missed meal; it is a way of life.

During the 2009-2010 school year, the Food for Kids Program (through the Regional Food Bank of Oklahoma) served 543 elementary age children here in Norman. When these children leave elementary school and move to middle school, there is not a program to feed them. Junior League of Norman is partnering with the Regional Food Bank of Oklahoma to change this.

Imagine your last meal was Friday's cafeteria lunch, and you won't get to eat again until Monday. Junior League of Norman provides backpacks containing enough food to feed them through the weekend.

Children that aren't hungry have better school attendance, better concentration in the classroom, and increased self-esteem.

Tribute

The *Sooner Sampler* was first published in 1987 and would not have been possible without the time and talents of many people – League members, restaurant owners, and Oklahoma personalities. Obviously, an endeavor of this magnitude, which involves hundreds of people, is not accomplished overnight. The idea for the cookbook first evolved in 1982 in the Project Development Committee, under the leadership of Sally Bratton and Betsy Anzalone.

After hours of research, exploration, and investigation into the efforts of numerous other organizations, all the collected data was passed on to the group responsible for collecting and testing recipes. Pam Clinton, chairman of the Cookbook Recipe Committee, along with Belinda Armstrong, Kathy Barrett, Manda Conklin, Susie Graves, Cheryl Martinsen, June Morgan, Suellen Tekell, and Randy Waddell, spent three years coordinating the testing of approximately 1,000 recipes submitted.

League members baked, sautéed, broiled, and simmered. Their families and friends sampled, devoured, praised, and critiqued. Evaluations of each recipe were compared and the final selections were made. Local restaurants and state personalities were asked to contribute their favorite recipes to be included in the original *Sooner Sampler.*

The first publication was an enormous success and sold 18,000 copies. Then in 2004, the 2003-2004 Provisional Class of the Junior League of Norman decided to bring back a revised edition of the original *Sooner Sampler.* The revised *Sooner Sampler* included new recipes from local favorites, as well as a new generation of Sooner notables.

We would like to give a huge thanks to all the League members who spearheaded the original *Sooner Sampler,* as well as to every member who has had a part of this project over the years. Without the efforts of all our members, past and present, this new 25th anniversary edition cookbook, *Simply Good Taste,* would not have been possible. We truly hope you enjoy your favorite recipes and find some new "tastes" to add to your collection.

Special Thank You To...

Modern Environment
Landscape

Mike and Libby Dillard

Belmar Golf Course

...

405 Imports

Birdie Floral

Carrington Lake Clubhouse

Frito Lay

Kerns

Kevin Bratcher

Dylan Hammett

Tim Kenney

Liz Massey

Darin and Jennifer Morgan

Megn Sparkman, Photography

Valorie Wakefield, Photography

The membership of the Junior League of Norman

2011–2012 Cookbook Committee

From left: Latoya Whitmire, Jessica Miller, Jackie Irwin, Katie Ihrig, Becca Vermelis, Kristie McKinney, and Liz Johnson. Not pictured: Jolene Curry and Kelly Parker

. . .

Katie Ihrig
Cookbook Chair

Becca Vermelis

Jackie Irwin

Jessica Miller

Jolene Curry

Kelly Parker

Kristie McKinney

Latoya Whitmire

Liz Johnson

. . .

Past Cookbook Committees

1987-1988 Cookbook Committee

Chris Purcell, Chairman
Jonella Frank, Vice Chairman
Paula Burrage, Typist
Barbara Clemens,
    Administrative Assistant

Linda English, Publicity
Barbara Huston, Finance
Vicky Kelsey, Special Projects
Jayne Marley, Marketing
Beth Ridgway, Editing

1988-1989 Cookbook Committee

Barbara Clemons, Chairman
Kris Akey
Kathy Blum

Joyce Brandes
Ginger Coker
Randy Waddell

1989-1990 Cookbook Committee

Ginger Coker, Chairman
Dawn Campbell
Janet Lanier

Kelley Murchison
Meg Newville
Tiffany Roper

1990-1991 Cookbook Committee

Julie Arvine
Debbie Bugg
Harriette Leigh
Kathleen Olmstead

Lee Ann Rogers
Mary Louise Symcox,
    Sustainer

1991-1992 Cookbook Committee

Debbie Bugg
Pam Deering
Sandra Gailey
Alexine Graves
Peggy Gutting

Cheryl Jones
Lee Ann Looman
Mary Powell
Mary Louise Symcox,
    Sustainer

2003-2004 Cookbook Committee
Provisional Class

Lisa Adams
Madelin Altom
Candance Anderson
Erin Barnhart
Cornelia Bass
Carol Bauman
Andrea Berryhill
Jennifer Brown
Rebecca Busey
Samantha Carmen
Jill Collier
Stephanie Corkins
Teka Cox
Jessica Delekta
Ashley Deming-Waslo
Brook Gann
Beth Harrison
Erin Hassen
Kari Hayes
Jennifer Heavner-Baker
Lisa Hussong
Celeste Johnson
Laura Kadechuk
Sarah Kielty
Toni Lee
Emily Leidner

Kelly Long
Deb Lupia
Joi Marcum
Andrea Marler
Amy McCall
Andrea Miles
Lacey Newby
Marissa Nuttle
Lindsi Owens
Elizabeth Oreb-Eastmond
Stephanie Roane
Chassidy Satterfield
Jennifer Schumaker
Amy Seagroves
Amy Sherry
Heather Smith-Gray
Sarah Soell
Jennie Sullivan
Cindy Teague
Melissa Thomas
Molly Thompson
Cheryl Todd
Allicyn Treat
Charla Uhles
Katy Ullrich
Amy Young

President's Letter

The Junior League of Norman continues its 38-year commitment to voluntarism and the continual improvement of the community through the efforts and leadership of the group's trained volunteers. Whether feeding hungry children, assisting teen parents in their efforts to finish school, supplying volunteers where needed or training more volunteers to further improve the community, the Junior League of Norman maintains a purpose that is exclusively educational and charitable.

Throughout the many years, women of the League, along with distinctive figures from the community, have been cooking delicious foods and sharing their special recipes to raise money that will further the Junior League of Norman's cause. Much like the ingredients in any recipe, each woman in our league brings something special and unique to the work we do. While individual contributions can be as varied as the recipes in this book, each of us donates our time, our heart, our talent and our hands to help build a better place to live for our families and friends. It's a labor of love for the Junior League of Norman, one that has helped us grow and continue to find new ways to helping those in need.

We think it is fitting that the proceeds from the sale of *Simply Good Taste* go directly towards our community projects to help them be more successful and to broaden their reach. Created with love and shared with a wealth of fond memories, we hope these tried-and-tested recipes bring happiness to your home and that the contribution made through your purchase of this book brings warmth to your heart. On behalf of the Junior League of Norman, Oklahoma, thank you for your generosity and your participation in the community.

Jennifer Burgell-Morgan

Jennifer Burgell Morgan
President, Junior League of Norman
2011 – 2012

People and Places

Our Culinary Collection features the following favorites from local celebrities and restaurants:

Barry Switzer

University of Oklahoma coaching legend, Barry Switzer, became head coach at Oklahoma in 1973, after serving as assistant coach and offensive coordinator for nine years. When Switzer retired from college coaching in 1989, he had a career record of 157-29-4, and his winning percentage of .837 is fourth best all-time. He coached the Dallas Cowboys from 1994-1997, winning Super Bowl XXX. He was inducted into the Oklahoma Sports Hall of Fame in 1990, the Oklahoma Heritage Hall of Fame in 1999, the College Football Hall of Fame in 2002 and received the Jim Thorpe Association's Lifetime Achievement Award in 2004. Switzer was known as a "player's coach," and even today his former players maintain a strong allegiance to their former mentor. While he is a highly visible personality in Oklahoma sports, business and public affairs, he also serves many worthwhile causes.

Lasagna, page 140

Bart Conner and Nadia Comaneci

Bart Conner is America's most decorated male gymnast, and the first American to win gold medals at every level of national and international competition. Conner was a three time member of the U.S. Olympic Team. He was inducted into the US Olympics Hall of Fame in 1991 and into the International Gymnastics Hall of Fame in 1996. Nadia Comaneci came into the hearts and minds of the world with her performance at the 1976 Olympics in Montreal, Canada, where she earned seven perfect tens, three gold medals, one bronze, one silver and countless fans. For her accomplishments, the two time Olympian was inducted into the International Gymnastics Hall of Fame. In April, 1996, Conner and Comaneci married in a Romanian state wedding, which was covered live on television throughout Romania. Today, Conner and Comaneci continue to travel the world promoting gymnastics, fitness and healthy lifestyles.

Eggplant Parmigiana, page 97

Billy Tubbs

A veteran coach who excelled at every level of coaching, Tubbs provided Sooner fans with an exciting style of basketball that generated great enthusiasm. His teams were annual contenders for the Big Eight crown and NCAA tournament play. His Oklahoma teams compiled a record of 333 wins and 132 losses. Tubbs developed a 641-340 record over his 31 years as a coach. He was known for his high scoring offenses, and full-court press defense.

Sherry Chicken, page 107

Bob Stoops

Since being named head coach in 1999, Bob Stoops has won the 2000 national championship, played for three more and captured eight Big 12 South crowns and seven Big 12 titles. Oklahoma has spent 30 weeks at No. 1 in the AP poll and a national-leading 20 weeks atop the BCS standings. Along the way, Stoops has picked up 17 coach of the year citations including eight on the national level. By embracing the rich tradition at the school and penning his own chapter in the Sooner lore, Stoops has authored a restoration that reaches far beyond the record book to the hearts of OU fans. He and his wife, Carol, have three children.

Sausage Stew, page 125

Cedric Jones

Cedric Jones was a member of the Sooner football squad from 1992 to 1995. He was drafted by the New York Giants in the first round of the NFL draft. He played five years for the Giants, including the 2000 Super Bowl Championship season. Cedric has been coaching since 2005 and is a centers/guards coach with Southern Nazarene University in Bethany, OK. He and his wife Susi reside in Norman with their three children: Cailey, Cameron, and Cash.

New York Giants Cheesecake, page 195

Dara Marie's Fine Baked Goods

(1420 N. Porter Avenue, Norman, OK)
John and Debbie Wullich opened their doors for business in August 1999. This quaint, family owned bakery provides delicious meals to go made from scratch in addition to a delectable array of sweets sure to make every mouth water. Dara Marie's is also the perfect place to find a gift for that special someone with their impressive offering of home decor and gift items.

Coconut Cream Pie, page 201

Dick Reynolds

Dick Reynolds has been a Ford dealer since 1952 and currently owns and operates Reynolds Ford-Lincoln-Mazda of Norman, Reynolds Ford-Lincoln of Edmond, and Reynolds Ford of Oklahoma City. He served two terms as mayor of Norman from 1986 to 1992.

Favorite New Potato Salad, page 173

Former Mayor Ron Henderson

Mayor Henderson is a lifelong Norman resident who has owned his own small businesses for close to 30 years. Henderson served on the Norman City Council from 1991 until 2001 and as mayor of Norman from 2001 to 2004.

Old Fashion Chocolate Sheet Cake, page 189

Brent Venables

One of the architects of what many consider the best defense in college football in the 2000's, Venables arrived at the University of Oklahoma in 1999 as co-defensive coordinator and linebackers coach. His linebackers have been key ingredients on a defense that has ranked among the nation's best in most statistical categories since the 2000 season. He and his wife, Julie, have two sons.

Bruschetta Chicken, page 109

Former First Lady of Oklahoma Kim Henry

Kim Henry is the wife of the 26th Governor of Oklahoma, Brad Henry. She was the First Lady of Oklahoma from January 13, 2003, to January 10, 2011.

She has devoted much of her life to education as a teacher. The former First Lady is currently serving on board of directors for the Oklahoma Medical Research Foundation and the Jasmine Moran Children's Museum. She previously served on the board of directors for Science Museum Oklahoma, Leadership Oklahoma, and the Oklahoma Foundation for Excellence. Henry is currently serving as the Executive Director of the Sarkeys Foundation, a private, charitable foundation dedicated to providing support through gifts and grants to Oklahoma's non-profit organizations.

Kim and Brad Henry have three daughters, Leah, Laynie and Baylee.

Shrimp Spring Rolls, page 30

Interurban Restaurant

(1150 Ed Noble Parkway, Norman, OK)
A local Oklahoma restaurant tradition since 1976, the founders opened the original Interurban Restaurant in Norman's "Interurban" Trolley Station. Interurban is a casual and fun concept featuring a wide variety of menu items catering to families, busy business professionals, young high school and college students, and baby boomers of all ages.

Our commitment to our customers back in 1976 is the same today: Good, fresh, quality food; reasonable prices; friendly and attentive service in clean and casual surroundings. All of our soups and sauces are prepared fresh on premise; we use 100% lean ground chuck; our steaks are aged a minimum of 21 days; we fry in 100% vegetable oil and offer a variety of "heart healthy" items. See you at the Urb!

Urban Sandwich, page 69

J.C. Watts

From leading his Oklahoma Sooners to two consecutive Orange Bowl titles, to his distinguished four-term career as a leading U.S. Congressman, J.C. Watts has proven he can deliver big wins in a diverse range of arenas. In 1999, he was named chair of the House Republican Conference, making him the fourth ranking Republican in the House of Representatives. He also created the J.C. Watts Foundation to focus on urban renewal and other charitable initiatives.

Oklahoma Mud Cake, page 189

Legends

(1313 West Lindsay Street, Norman, OK)
Upon walking in the doors at Legends, you are tempted by the beautiful desserts on display. Equally as pleasing are the many menu selections that include fresh seafood, pasta, beef and daily specials, representative of current trends in eating. Legends holds a three star rating in the Forbes Travel Guide (formerly Mobil Travel Guide) and a three diamond rating with the AAA Travel Guide. Their homemade desserts have been recognized by Bon Appetit and Southern Living magazines, and are a recipient of the Oklahoma Beef Commission's "Silver Knife Award". In various newspaper polls they have been voted Best Norman Restaurant, Best Sunday Brunch, Best Desserts, Best Chocolate, Most Elegant Norman Restaurant, Best Wine List, Best Norman Gourmet Restaurant, Best Place to take Out-of-town Guests, Best First Date Restaurant, Best Caterer, and Top 21 restaurants in the OKC Metro Area.

Spinach Quiche, page 71
Poppyseed Dressing, page 74
Filet of Beef with Green Madagascar Peppercorns, page 133
Autumn Nut Torte, page 200

Luciano's

(Once located at 1816 West Lindsey Street, Norman, OK)
Italian Cuisine served in an elegant, yet relaxed atmosphere was the mark of Luciano's. Diners could choose from pasta, seafood, chicken or beef dishes prepared "a la Luciano."

Veal Marsala, page 144

Mark Amspacher

Growing up in the family-owned grocery, which started in 1936, Mark knows all about food. He put that knowledge to work for him creating his championship chili, which repeatedly won first place honors in the state chili cook off. Mark owned, The Diner, which was featured on the Food Network's *Diners, Drive-ins and Dives*. Mark passed away Feb 1. 2010.

State Championship Chili, page 145

The Mont

(1300 Classen Boulevard, Norman, OK)
Located in the building that housed The Monterrey Restaurant, a college hangout of past generations, The Mont offers a selection of Mexican food, sandwiches, steaks, appetizers, and salads. You can enjoy your meals indoors in historic surroundings or outdoors on the heated patio.

Hot Bean Dip, page 43

Nonna's

(1 Mickey Mantle Drive, Oklahoma City, OK)
Step into a restaurant reminiscent of a small European sidewalk cafe located in the heart of Bricktown. Nonna's is the perfect place to dine in Bricktown whether you are looking for casual or fine dining.

Chocolate Cake, page 187

O Asian Fusion

(105 12th Avenue SE, Norman, OK)
O Asian Fusion is owned by JLN Past President Stephanie O'Hara. "O" offers all things Asian - including sushi, stir frys, noodles, made from scratch soups and appetizers to steaks, fine sake and wine and exotic cocktails. Their award-winning food is cooked to order using the freshest, local ingredients.

O Asian Fusion's Spicy Shrimp Noodle Soup, page 91

Pinks

(Once located at 607 West Boyd Street, Norman, OK)
This cozy neighborhood restaurant served three meals
a day. You could enjoy anything from omelets to Eggs
Benedict for breakfast and select from a range of
homemade soups, sandwiches and unique specials for
lunch and dinner.

....

Chicken a La Reine Soup, page 88

Point of Grace

Shelley Breen, Terry Jones, Heather Payne, and Denise
Jones were barely out of college when they began their
journey as Point of Grace. Nearly two decades later, they
have one platinum and five gold albums to their credit.
They also have 24 consecutive Number 1 singles, 14 Dove
awards and two Grammy nods. Norman claims three-
fourths of the original members of this fabulous group as
their own, since Terry, Heather, and Denise are all Norman
High School graduates.

....

Garden Party Fondue, page 43

Regent G.T. Blankenship

Regent Blankenship was appointed to the Board of
Regents by Governor Henry Bellmon in the spring of
1990, and was reappointed in 1997 by Governor Frank
Keating. He attended the University of Oklahoma receiving
Bachelor of Arts and LL.B. degrees. In 1960, Mr. Blankenship
was elected to the State House of Representatives and
served as Minority Floor Leader from 1964-66. He was
elected Attorney General of the State of Oklahoma and
served from 1966 to 1970. Mr. Blankenship has been in the
private practice of law in Oklahoma City, is Board Chairman
of the Bank of Nichols Hills, has served as Chairman of the
State Centennial Committee, was on the Board of Directors
for the U.S. Olympic Festival, and has been active in the
Oklahoma City Chamber of Commerce.

....

Oven Stew, page 144

Steve Owens

Steve Owens was a two-time All-American football player
at the University of Oklahoma. In 1969, he won the Heisman
trophy. He was drafted by the Detroit Lions in 1970 where
he became the first player on a Detroit Lions team to rush
for over 1,000 yards. He was chosen All-Pro in 1971 and
elected to the College Football Hall of Fame in 1991.

....

Sausage Egg Casserole, page 66
Favorite Apple Pie, page 204

Sherri Coale

Head Coach Sherri Coale brings a winning attitude to the women's basketball program at the University of Oklahoma. Under her direction, the Sooners have sparked excitement for women's basketball across the state and nation. During the 15 years as Head Coach her accomplishments include ten Big 12 championship trophies that reside at the Lloyd Noble Center. All ten, six regular season and four postseason, have come since the 1999-00 season. The collection of titles is tops in the Big 12. Coale, grew up in Healdton, Oklahoma. She and her husband, Dane, have two children, Colton and Chandler.

Chocolate Chip Cheese Ball, page 194

Steve Nunno

Steve Nunno is one of the most successful gymnastics coaches in the United States. Gymnasts from his Dynamo club in Oklahoma City have won more national and international medals than any other club in the country. Nunno coached many junior national champions. Nunno was head coach for the winning U.S. women's gymnastics team at the Pan American games and head coach at the 1994 Goodwill Games where the entire U.S. women's gymnastics team were all from his Dynamo club. He has been honored as "Coach of the Year" numerous times. He is now focused on the collegiate game as the head coach of the University of Oklahoma's women's gymnastics team. Nunno, who still owns two Dynamo gymnastics clubs in the Oklahoma City area, lives in Edmond with his wife, Laurie, and their three children.

Mushrooms Parma, page 30

The Union Banquet and Catering Service

(900 Asp Avenue, Norman, OK)
The Union was completed in 1928 as a memorial to the students, faculty, and staff of the University who fought and died in World War I.

The Union has more than 26 meeting and activity rooms and eight dining kiosks. The Meacham Auditorium has 400 seats, and the Molly Shi Boren Ballroom, on the third floor, seats up to 500 banquet guests.

Whether it is serving a banquet for two hundred or catering a small reception, the Union can handle it. With an extensive menu of everything from appetizers to elegant wedding cakes, the Union has the perfect culinary treat for any gathering.

Roast Rack of Lamb, page 127

Victory Gymnastics

(5721 Huettner Court, Norman, OK)
Victory gymnastics opened its doors on October 16, 2000 with only one student and two goals; to build great athletes and change children's lives by challenging them to discover God's great destiny for them. Today, Victory gymnastics is home to more than 1,000 athletes, including many top gymnasts in the state, region, and nation. In 2005, Victory Academy, a private Christian school was opened to produce champions and allow dedicated athletes the opportunity to train and compete nationally and worldwide. Because of the success and tightly run organization of Victory Gymnastics, they have added satellite programs of Victory Cheer and Victory Tae Kwon Do. Victory is a 501(c)(3) not-for-profit organization. The Hope Foundation for Aspiring Youth governs Victory Athletics.

Hawaiian Chicken, page 122

Wine and Food Pairings

Rules are meant to be broken right? But there are some guidelines to stick to so you're not left with a disappointing dinner. Trust us; poached fish does not go with Zinfandel. The fish can make the wine taste bitter and/or metallic.

Acidity: The acidity in the wine should be equal to the acidity in the dish. If not, the wine will taste dull. Because red wines lack acidity, this means sticking primarily to white wines if you're eating salad, lemon chicken, or vinegar-based dishes. (A few young reds will stand up to a bit of lemon, including Beaujolais and good Lambrusco from Italy, a light fizzy red wine made from indigenous varietals; just serve them chilled.)

Bitterness: if you love bitter foods (arugula, broccoli, endive), service them with tannic wines. The bitter edge of the tannins will marry with the bitter foods. Bitter tannins will wreak havoc with fish, and some vegetables, so serve a less tannic Pinot Noir with your salmon and save the Cabernet Sauvignon and Merlot for something richer.

Salt: Tannic wines will make food seem saltier. Salt also accentuates alcohol in wine, so remember that if you're seasoning a dish you plan to serve with a big, tannic wine.

Sweets: The basic rule is that the wine has to be at least as sweet as (or sweeter than) the food. If it's not, the wine will taste tart and thin. The sweetest treats can go with heavy, sweet dessert wines like Muscats from France and Australia, Sherry, and late-harvest Semillons and Rieslings. Poached fruit and fruit tarts usually pair with everything.

Spice: Spicy foods (curries, chili peppers, and so on) will make wines seem more alcoholic. For spicy food, stick to sweet wines that can counteract the spice. Sweet wines not meaning dessert wines; wines that have more fruit and may have the impression of being sweet even though there is little or no residual sugar. Whites such as Gewürztraminer, Riesling, Chenin Blanc, and Pinot Gris pair well with light, spicy dishes such as Thai food, while soft fruity reds like Merlot and Beaujolais go well with heavier, sauce-driven spiced dishes.

Like with Like: If you are eating light food, choose lighter-style wines. The same goes for rich food; this is called the complementary approach to wine and food pairing. Balance is key to allow the wine and food magic to happen. (Although a few sweet/dessert wine combos turn that rule on its head; some desserts require lighter wines.) Another easy way to approach this principle is to think of the region of the wine and the food; the food and wine from a region are indelibly intertwined. The rich, tangy pork and charcuterie of Alsace, France, is served with the dry, elegant Riesling, while the tomato based and rustic meat dishes of Tuscany, Italy, are paired with lively Sangiovese. There's a reason some pairings have been around for thousands of years.

Sparkling to the Rescue: Thanks to the acidity and the bubbles, dry sparkling wine goes with everything, especially foods with vinegar, lemon, capers, tomatoes, and vinaigrettes. (The one thing dry sparkling wine does not go with is sweets! Champagne and wedding cake don't mix.)

Cheese and Wine: Cheese and wine have been served together since the invention of the cocktail party, so most people think these two are a natural pair. But it's not always wine and roses. Some Cheeses are so strong that they will emphasize the tannins in the red wine and turn you off cheese and wine forever, while some white wines are overpowered by strong cheeses. The most basic (and successful) pairings include Sauvignon Blanc with goat cheese, Chardonnay with Cheddar, vintage Champagne with Parmigiano-Reggiano, Stilton with vintage Port, and Roquefort with Sauternes.

Wine and Chocolate: People love to pair wine with chocolate although few combos actually work. Fortified wines like Port generally are seamless pairing with chocolate: Rich, velvety Port can match up to intense chocolate, as dessert wines like Brachetto d'Acqui from Italy can cut through the rich texture and add a zip to a chocolate dessert. Some chocolate lovers serve Cabernet Sauvignon, and while it can work, make sure you choose a fruit Cabernet (rather than an earthy, more herbaceous one).

HERE IS A SUGGESTED LIST OF TYPES OF DISHES AND WHAT TYPES OF WINES WOULD COMPLEMENT THEM THE BEST:

Beef: Zinfandel, Beaujolais, Cotes du Rhone, Cabernet Sauvignon, Pinot Noir, Syrah, Medoc

Cheeses: Merlot, Cabernet, Chardonnay, Grenache Rose

Chicken: Riesling, Merlot, Chianti, Chardonnay

Corned Beef: Beaujolais, Dolcetto, Alsatian Pinot Gris

Duck / Goose: Pinot Noir, Rhone, Cabernet Sauvignon

Egg dishes: Rose, Champagne

Fish: Sauvignon Blanc, Soave, Loire whites, Pinot Noir

Ham: Beaujolais, Zinfandel, Riesling, Gewurztraminer, Chenin Blanc

Lamb: Spanish Rioja, Cabernet Sauvignon, Pinot Noir, fine Italian Reds, St-Emilion

Pork: Pinot Grigio, Chardonnay, Chianti, Merlot

Scallops: French Hermitage blanc, Grand cru Chablis, German Kabinett, Pacific Northwest Austrian gruner vertliners, Spanish Rias Baixas, Portuguese white Vinho verde, Graves and Burgundies, New World chardonnays, German Ausleses and Spatleses

Shellfish: Sauvignon Blanc, Riesling, Chardonnay, Champagne, White Graves

Turkey: Beaujolais, Riesling, Vouvray, Alsatian Gewurztraminer, Champagne, White Graves

Veal: Gavi, Vernaccia, Chardonnay, Chianti, white Bordeaux, white Burgundy

Vegetarian: Pinot Gris, Sauvignon Blanc, Zinfandel, Chianti

Beverages

Alcoholic

Frozen Margaritas

· 16 oz. can of limeade concentrate
· 6 oz. beer (fill limeade can)
· 6 oz. tequila (fill limeade can)
· 1.5 oz. triple sec (optional)
· Ice

Put limeade, beer, and tequila in blender. Fill blender with ice and mix until slushy. Serve immediately.

Serves 4-6.

Citrus Mimosas

· 1 c. prepared strawberry daiquiri mix
· 6 oz. frozen orange juice concentrate, thawed
· ¾ c. water
· 1 c. grapefruit juice
· 3 oz. frozen lemonade, thawed
· Champagne

Mix first five ingredients and chill. Pour mix into punch bowl and add champagne.

Sangria

· 6 c. (1 bottle) dry red or white wine
· 2 cans lemon-lime soda
· 3 c. orange juice
· 1 c. brandy
· ¼ c. sugar (optional, if you like it sweeter)
· ¼ c. triple sec
· ¼ c. Grand Marnier or Liqueur 43
· 4 Tbsp. grenadine
· Juice of 1 lemon
· Juice of 2 limes
· Orange, lime, and lemon slices, for garnish

Combine all ingredients in large pitcher. Refrigerate for at least 30 minutes. Serve over ice and garnish with additional slices of fruit, if desired. Can be prepared in advance, but don't add soda until almost ready to serve — it will lose its fizz.

Serves 4-6

BEVERAGES

Alcoholic

Champagne Punch

- 1 ¼ c. water
- 1 ¼ c. pineapple juice
- 1 (6 oz.) can frozen lemon juice (or lemonade concentrate) plus 2 cans of water
- 3 (6 oz.) cans frozen orange juice plus 2 cans of water
- 1 ½ c. sugar
- 1 bottle champagne (or ginger ale), chilled
- 1 pt. frozen strawberries, partially thawed

Mix well all ingredients except champagne and strawberries. Add strawberries and champagne just before serving.

Serves 20 (6 oz. servings).

Mulled Wine Punch

- 1 qt. cranberry juice
- ½ c. sugar
- ½ c. brown sugar
- ½ cinnamon stick
- 6 whole cloves
- 6 whole allspice berries
- 1 bottle Burgundy wine

Mix cranberry juice and sugars in large saucepan. Tie spices in cheese cloth or put in a tea ball. Add to cranberry juice. Heat until boiling. Reduce heat. Simmer for 5 minutes. Discard spices. Add wine. Heat until piping hot but DO NOT BOIL. Can be made in advance and refrigerated.

Serves 8-10.

Non-Alcoholic

Coffee Punch

· 12 c. coffee
· 1 c. sugar
· 1 tsp. vanilla
· ½ gal. vanilla or chocolate ice cream
· 1 c. whipped topping
· Maraschino cherries, drained

At least 2 hours before serving, brew coffee. Add sugar and vanilla while still hot. Stir until dissolved. Cool at least 1 ½ hours.

Half an hour before serving, stir in ice cream and whipped topping. Garnish as desired with whipped topping and cherries.

Fancy Punch

· 2 liter lemon-lime soda
· 1 can pink lemonade concentrate
· 1 bag frozen mixed berries

Mix lemon-lime soda and lemonade concentrate. Add berries. Serve in punch bowl.

Pine-Orange-Banana Punch

· 4 c. sugar
· 6 c. water
· 46 oz. pineapple juice
· 46 oz. orange juice
· 5 ripe bananas, mashed
· Juice of 2 lemons
· 3 qts. ginger ale

Mix all ingredients except ginger ale in a large freezable container. Place in the freezer and leave about 2 days.

Remove from freezer about 2 hours before serving. Pour into punch bowl and add ginger ale to make slushy.

Non-Alcoholic

Peach Punch

- · 1 can peach nectar
- · 1 liter ginger ale
- · 1 can lemonade concentrate, prepared
  according to directions
- · Orange sherbet

Mix first three ingredients together and top with orange sherbet.

Pink Lady Punch

- · 4 c. cranberry juice cocktail
- · 1 ½ c. granulated sugar
- · 4 c. pineapple juice
- · 2 qts. chilled ginger ale

Add cranberry juice to sugar. Stir until dissolved. Add pineapple juice and ginger ale. Chill.

Can be prepared ahead and refrigerated.

Makes 32 servings.

Red Punch

- · 1 can pineapple juice
- · 3 envelopes cherry Kool-Aid®
- · 3 cups sugar
- · 1 liter lemon-lime soda
- · 2 liters ginger ale
- · Raspberry sherbet

Thoroughly mix pineapple juice, Kool-Aid®, and sugar and place in freezer until slushy.

When ready to serve, add lemon-lime soda, ginger ale, and top with sherbet.

Appetizers

Zucchini Oven Chips

· ¼ c. breadcrumbs
· ¼ c. Parmesan cheese
· ¼ tsp. seasoned salt
· ¼ tsp. garlic powder
· ¼ tsp. pepper
· 2 Tbsp. skim milk
· 2 ½ c. zucchini, sliced ¼-inch thick
· Cooking spray

Preheat oven to 425°.

Combine breadcrumbs, Parmesan, seasoned salt, garlic powder, and pepper. Mix well.

Place milk in a shallow bowl. Dip zucchini in milk, and then dredge in breadcrumb mixture. Place on sprayed baking stone.

Bake at 425° for 30 minutes. Serve immediately.

Serves 4.

Baked Curried Zucchini

· 1 egg
· 1 c. flour
· 1 tsp. salt
· 1 tsp. curry powder
· ¼ tsp. pepper
· 3 medium zucchini – cut into ¼-inch slices
· Olive oil

Preheat oven to 400°.

Beat egg and set aside. Combine flour, salt, curry powder, and pepper in a shallow dish.

Dip zucchini slices in egg, then roll in seasoned flour. Arrange slices on a greased baking sheet. Sprinkle generously with olive oil (can also sprinkle more curry powder if desired).

Bake at 400° until crisp and golden about 20 minutes, turning once. Drain and serve immediately.

Steve Nunno's Mushroom Parma

· 1 lb. fresh mushrooms
· ½ c. freshly shredded Parmesan cheese
· ¼ c. shredded Mozzarella cheese
· ¼ c. green onions, chopped
· ½ c. melted butter

Remove stems of mushrooms and finely chop stems. Combine stems, cheeses, green onions, and butter. Fill mushroom caps with mixture. Place on rack of broiler pan and broil 2 to 3 minutes or until slightly crusted.

Serve hot.

Serves 4.

First Lady's Shrimp Spring Rolls

· 2 Tbsp. soy sauce
· 1 tsp. sugar
· 1 tsp. cornstarch
· ¼ tsp. salt
· ¼ tsp. pepper
· ¾ lb. peeled, deveined, and lightly sautéed shrimp
· 1 package egg roll wrappers
· ½ Tbsp. ground ginger
· 1 ½ c. shredded cabbage
· 2 - 3 Tbsp. vegetable oil
· 1 clove garlic, minced
· ½ c. thinly sliced green onions
· ¾ c. diced water chestnuts

Combine soy sauce, sugar, cornstarch, salt, and pepper in a small bowl. Mix well and set aside.

Combine green onions, water chestnuts and cabbage in a small bowl. Toss to mix and set aside.

Heat 1 Tbsp. oil in a large skillet or wok. Add garlic and ginger. Stir and sauté for 1 minute. Add half the vegetable mixture and stir fry until slightly softened (about 30 seconds to 1 minute). Push to side of pan and repeat with remaining vegetable mixture, then remove from pan. Add 1 Tbsp. oil to pan and heat. Add ½ the shrimp and stir-fry until cooked. Push to side of pan and repeat with remaining shrimp, using more oil if necessary. Return vegetable mixture to pan with shrimp and pour soy sauce mixture over all. Cook, stirring constantly, until mixture thickens (about 1 ½ minutes). Remove from pan and cool.

When cooled, wrap in egg roll wrappers and fry until wrap is crispy. Remove and top with plum sauce.

Plum Sauce
· ½ tsp. dry mustard
· 1 Tbsp. vinegar
· ½ c. plum preserves

Dissolve dry mustard in vinegar. Stir into plum preserves until smooth.

Cheese Wontons with Hot Sauce

· ¾ c. shredded cheddar cheese
· 2 Tbsp. chopped green chiles, drained
· 2 dozen wonton skins
· Peanut oil

Place 1 ½ tsp. cheese and ¼ tsp. green chiles in the center of each wonton skin. Fold into desired shape, brushing edges with water to seal.

Heat oil to 375° in a wok or large skillet. Place wontons in hot oil and fry 30 seconds on each side, or until golden brown.

Drain on paper towels. Serve immediately with hot sauce (recipe below).

Hot Sauce
· ⅓ c. onion, chopped
· 1 clove garlic, minced
· 1 Tbsp. vegetable oil
· ½ c. chopped tomatoes, drained
· 1 Tbsp. jalapeño peppers, chopped
· ¼ tsp. ground cumin
· ¼ tsp. salt
· 1 (8 oz.) can tomato sauce
· 1 ½ Tbsp. vinegar

Sauté onion and garlic in hot oil until tender. Add remaining ingredients and cook until heated through.

Serves about 2 dozen.

Mexican Torte

· 2 eggs, beaten
· 2 Tbsp. flour
· ½ tsp. salt
· ⅓ c. milk
· 1 (4 oz.) can chopped green chiles
· ½ lb. sharp cheddar cheese, grated
· ½ lb. Monterey Jack cheese, grated

Preheat oven to 350°.

Mix all ingredients. Pour into a buttered 9×13-inch pan. Bake at 350° for 35 to 40 minutes.

Cut into squares and serve hot.

Serves 4-6.

Mini Quiches

· 1 (8 oz.) can refrigerated butter flake rolls
· 1 (2 ½ oz.) can tiny shrimp, drained
· 1 egg, slightly beaten
· ½ c. half and half
· 1 Tbsp. brandy
· ½ tsp. salt
· Dash of pepper
· 1 tsp. chopped pimiento
· ½ tsp. parsley flakes
· ½ c. shredded Gruyere or cheddar cheese

Preheat oven to 375°.

Generously grease 24 miniature muffin cups. Separate dough into 12 pieces. Divide each roll in half. Press dough into muffin cups, covering bottom and sides.

Divide shrimp evenly among shells. In a small bowl combine egg, half and half, brandy, salt, pepper, pimiento, and parsley flakes. Spoon approximately 1 Tbsp. mixture into each shell. Sprinkle with cheese.

Bake at 375° for 20 minutes or until puffy and light golden brown. Cool slightly. Remove from muffin cups. Serve warm.

Note – Can be prepared in advance and frozen until ready to use. To reheat, place on cookie sheet; bake at 375° for 10 to 12 minutes.

Crab Crumpets

· 3 packages English muffins
· 1 lb. grated sharp cheddar cheese
· 2 (6 ½ oz.) cans crabmeat
· 1 small onion, finely chopped
· 2 c. mayonnaise
· 1 tsp. prepared mustard
· ¾ c. white wine
· 2 Tbsp. lemon juice
· Dash of each – seasoned salt, pepper, and garlic powder

Mix all ingredients together, except muffins. Cut muffin halves into halves or fourths. Spread mixture on top of each. Broil until topping is bubbly and golden brown.

Note – To prepare in advance, place on cookie sheets and freeze. When frozen, place in plastic bags until ready to broil.

Pita Bread Snacks

· 1 c. mayonnaise
· ½ c. Parmesan cheese
· 2 green onions, finely chopped
· Garlic powder, to taste
· 3 pita bread slices

Preheat oven to 350°.

Mix first four ingredients. Cut pita bread into 6 pie-shaped wedges and separate each wedge into two pieces. Spread mixture thinly on bread.

Bake at 350° for 15 to 20 minutes or until golden brown.

Makes 36 snacks.

Ricotta with Dates and Pistachios Bruschetta

· 8 bread rounds from a baguette, sliced ½-inch thick
· ¼ c. pistachios, chopped
· ¼ c. dates, chopped
· ½ c. (8 Tbsp.) whole milk ricotta
· Honey, as needed

Preheat oven to 375°.

Toast bread rounds until crispy, about 7 minutes. Toast pistachios on a baking sheet for 1 minute, stir, and toast another minute or until nuts just start to brown (be careful not to burn them).

Allow bread rounds and pistachios to cool for a few minutes.

Assemble bruschetta by spreading 1 Tbsp. of ricotta on each bread round, then sprinkle pistachios and dates over the ricotta, and drizzle a little honey over the top.

Pan Con Tomate
(Crusty Bread with Tomato)

· 1 loaf thick-sliced crusty bread
· 4 - 5 ripe tomatoes
· Extra-virgin olive oil
· Manchego cheese slices (Spanish cheese)
· Serrano ham (or Prosciutto) (optional)
· Salt and pepper, to taste

Cut slices of bread about ⅔-inch thick. Cut tomatoes in half and rub pulp slowly into both slices of the bread slices to color the bread. Sprinkle both slices of the bread with salt. Drizzle both sides of the bread with olive oil and top with Manchego cheese slices. Serve with very thin slices of Serrano ham or Prosciutto if desired.

Serves 4 - 6.

Shrimp Rounds

· 1 c. butter
· 1 ½ c. flour
· ½ c. sour cream
· ½ c. grated sharp cheddar cheese

Cut butter into flour. Mixture will be small crumbs. Stir in sour cream and cheddar cheese. Divide dough in half, wrap in wax paper. Chill overnight.

Roll out half of dough on floured surface. With a fancy 2-inch cutter, cut out sixty rounds. From these, using a 1-inch round hors d'oeuvre cutter, cut a 1-inch circle out of the center. Add the centers back to dough and cut out thirty 2-inch rounds. Place the solid thirty rounds on ungreased baking sheet. Brush with milk. Top each with two rounds with centers removed. Brush with milk between layers.

Bake at 350° for 22 to 25 minutes. Cool on wire rack. Just before serving, fill with shrimp mixture (recipe below).

Shrimp Mixture
· 1 (8 oz.) package cream cheese, softened
· ¼ c. milk
· 1 tsp. lemon juice
· 1 tsp. Worcestershire sauce
· ¼ tsp. dill weed
· 4 ½ to 5 oz. small shrimp, cooked and divided

Beat cream cheese and milk. Add lemon juice, Worcestershire sauce, and dill weed. Stir in half the shrimp. Reserve thirty small shrimp and chill. Spoon mixture into pastry rounds. Garnish with shrimp. Sprinkle with dill weed.

Serves 30.

English Crab Bites

· 1 can (7 ½ oz.) white crab meat
· 1 jar (5 oz.) Kraft® Old English cheddar cheese
· 1 stick butter or margarine, softened
· 2 Tbsp. mayonnaise
· ½ tsp. garlic powder (or fresh grated)
· ½ tsp. onion powder (or fresh grated)
· ⅛ c. cooking sherry
· Tabasco® dashes or cayenne pepper, to taste
· 6 English muffins

Blend first eight ingredients together. Split muffins and spread generously over halves. Freeze on cookie sheets for about 45 minutes to 1 hour. Transfer to freezer bag and keep frozen until ready to serve. (At this point you can transfer to freezer bag and save in your freezer up to 2 months)

To prepare, preheat oven to 450°. While oven is preheating, cut each muffin half into fourths. Place on cookie sheet and bake 8 -12 minutes. Serve immediately.

Suzanne's Crab Appetizer

· 12 oz. cream cheese, softened
· 2 Tbsp. Worcestershire sauce
· 1 Tbsp. lemon juice
· 2 Tbsp. mayonnaise
· 1 small onion, grated
· Dash of garlic salt
· 1 bottle chili sauce
· 1 (6 ½ oz.) can crab, drained
· Parsley, for garnish

Layer 1: Mix cream cheese, Worcestershire, lemon juice, mayonnaise, and onion. Spread on shallow plate.

Layer 2: Pour chili sauce over layer 1.

Layer 3: Spread crab over layer 2. Garnish with parsley. Serve with snack crackers.

Note – Men love this one. It always goes fast!

Texas Caviar

· 1 can black-eyed peas
· 1 can black beans
· 1 can diced tomatoes
· 1 small can chopped jalapeños
· 1 green bell pepper, chopped
· 1 bunch of green onions, chopped
· 1 tsp. garlic, minced
· 1 cup Zesty Italian dressing
· Fresh cilantro, red pepper flakes, Tabasco®,
    salt and pepper, to taste

Drain the peas, beans, tomatoes, and jalapeños; combine
with other ingredients. Refrigerate overnight.

Serve with tortilla chips or crackers.

Serves 4.

Loaded Dip

· 6 oz. bacon, cooked and finely crumbled
· 1 c. light mayonnaise
· 1 c. light sour cream
· 1 medium tomato or 2 Roma tomatoes, seeded and diced
· 2 c. shredded mild cheddar cheese
· 3 green scallions, chopped
· Salt and pepper, to taste

Mix all ingredients, except scallions, and refrigerate at least
1 hour before serving.

Spread scallions evenly on top just before serving. Serve
with chips, French bread, and/or veggies.

Black Olive Dip

· 2 (4 oz.) cans chopped black olives
· 1 can chopped green chiles
· 2 large tomatoes, chopped
· 1 bunch green onions, chopped
· 3 Tbsp. oil
· 2 Tbsp. vinegar
· 2 ½ Tbsp. Greek seasoning

Mix ingredients and chill. Serve with tortilla chips. Dip gets better the longer it sits.

Boursin

· 2 (8 oz.) packages cream cheese
· 4 oz. butter, softened
· 1 tsp. oregano
· ¼ tsp. dill
· ¼ tsp. basil
· ¼ tsp. thyme
· ¼ tsp. marjoram
· ¼ tsp. cracked pepper
· 2 cloves garlic

Process all ingredients in blender or food processor until smooth. Refrigerate at least 4 hours. Serve as a spread with crackers.

Note–To make cheese ball, omit pepper from the recipe and roll the ball in cracked pepper.

Spicy Cheese Ball

· 16 oz. cream cheese, softened
· 2 oz. ripe black olives, chopped
· 3 oz. salad green olives, chopped
· ¼ medium onion, chopped
· 2 tsp. Tabasco® sauce
· 1 c. finely grated cheddar cheese
· Chopped pecans

In large mixing bowl, combine cream cheese, olives, onion, Tabasco® sauce and cheddar cheese. Mix until fluffy. Cover mixture and chill slightly.

On wax paper, roll mixture into ball, and then roll ball in the chopped pecans. Wrap in plastic wrap. Chill at least 2 hours in refrigerator.

Dee's Famous Salsa

· 1 c. chopped onion
· 2 (14.5 oz.) cans diced tomatoes
· ½ c. stemmed cilantro
· 2 Tbsp. chopped garlic
· 1 Tbsp. cumin powder
· 2 fresh jalapeños, chopped
· 2 fresh serrano peppers, chopped
· 1 Tbsp. black pepper
· 1 Tbsp. salt
· 1 tsp. chipotle powder

Pulse ingredients in blender until desired consistency. Be careful not to blend too long.

Serve with corn chips.

Delicioso Easy Salsa

· 2 (28 oz.) cans whole tomatoes
· ½ bunch cilantro
· 1 (28 oz.) can tomatillos or 6 - 8 fresh tomatillos
      roasted in oven for 20 min. until soft at 450°
· 1 medium onion
· 2 green bell peppers or poblano peppers
· 1 - 4 fresh whole jalapeños, to taste
· 1 chopped, peeled mango
· ½ - 1 c. ketchup (depending on desired thickness)
· ¼ c. lime juice
· 1 (28 oz.) can petite diced tomatoes
      (don't put in processor)
· Salt, to taste

Roughly chop all fresh ingredients and put the WHOLE canned tomatoes, cilantro, tomatillos, onion, peppers, jalapeños and mango into a food processor in batches and blend to desired consistency. Mix all the ingredients in a very large bowl, add salt if needed, and transfer to containers.

Note–Keeps for 2 to 3 weeks in the fridge. Makes enough to give some away!

Green Apple Salsa

· 1 lemon
· 1 white onion
· 1 lime
· 1 poblano pepper
· 3 oz. honey
· 2 Granny Smith apples
· 3 oz. fresh cilantro

Squeeze as much juice and pulp from lemon and lime as possible. (Add zest if desired.) Add honey and mix well. Peel, core, and dice apples to very small (.2 inches) Peel 1st apple, and add diced pieces to mix. Then peel the 2nd apple. (This keeps them from turning brown.) Peel and dice onion to same size of apple. Add to mix. Dice poblano to same size. Add to mix. Finely chop cilantro. Add to mix. Mix everything well.

Serve immediately or let sit in fridge overnight to let the flavors blend together.

Serve with chips.

Note–Could also be served over fish or pork.

Cyndie's Fruit Salsa with Cinnamon Chips

Salsa:
· 1 c. frozen or fresh strawberries, thawed and mashed
· 1 ½ c. fresh strawberries, diced
· 2 medium apples, peeled and diced
· 2 kiwis, peeled and diced
· 1 mango, peeled and diced
· 1 orange, peeled and diced
· 2 Tbsp. brown sugar
· 2 Tbsp. apple jelly
· Fresh mint leaves, julienned, for garnish (optional)

Mix all ingredients together and refrigerate until ready to serve.

Note – You can use any fruit or berries you have on hand, just not bananas–they will turn brown too quickly and ruin the color of the salsa.

Cinnamon & Sugar Chips:
· 12 flour tortillas
· Water
· 2 Tbsp. sugar
· 1 tsp. ground cinnamon

Preheat oven to 475°.

In a small bowl, mix cinnamon, and sugar together. Lightly brush tortillas with water (don't get them too wet-you just want the sugar mix to stick). Cut tortillas into 6 to 8 triangles each, and put on cookie sheet. Sprinkle with the sugar mixture and bake at 475° for 5 to 7 minutes or until chips become crispy.

Serve chips with the fruit salsa.

Kids' Warm Peanut-Caramel Dip

· ½ c. peanut butter
· 2 Tbsp. caramel ice cream topping
· 2 Tbsp. milk
· 1 large apple, sliced
· 4 large pretzel rods, halved

Combine peanut butter, caramel topping, and milk in a saucepan. Cook over low heat until mixture is melted. Serve dip with apple slices and pretzels.

Pepperoni Dip

· 8 oz. cream cheese, softened
· 2 c. sour cream
· 1 can green chiles, undrained
· ½ c. green onions, chopped
· 1 tsp. of Creole seasoning
· 3.5 oz. pepperoni, chopped
· ½ c. chopped pecans

Preheat oven to 350°.

Mix together first 6 ingredients. Top with pecans. Bake at 350° for 20 minutes.

Serve with crackers or pasta chips.

Buffalo Chicken Dip

· 16 oz. cream cheese, softened
· 8 oz. hot sauce (like Tabasco®)
· ¾ c. chopped celery
· 2 c. cooked shredded chicken
· 1 c. shredded cheese (I use quesadilla cheese, but you can use anything)
· Blue cheese crumbles, to taste (optional)

Preheat oven to 350°.

Mix all ingredients in a casserole dish, top with the shredded cheese, and bake at 350° for 30 minutes.

Serve warm with crackers or celery sticks.

Beef Picadillo

- · 1 lb. ground beef
- · 1 (16 oz.) can tomatoes
- · 1 (11 oz.) can Rotel® tomatoes
- · 3 green onions, chopped fine
- · ¾ c. pimiento, diced
- · ¾ c. almonds, toasted and diced
- · ¼ tsp. oregano
- · 1 tsp. salt
- · ¼ tsp. pepper
- · 2 cloves garlic, minced (or ½ tsp. liquid garlic)
- · 1 (6 oz.) can tomato paste

Brown meat and drain grease. Add all other ingredients. Cook on low for 30 minutes. Stir occasionally. Serve warm.

Note – This is best served with corn chips or something that does not break easily. Can be prepared ahead and frozen.

Sausage and Mushroom Dip

- · 1 lb. spicy ground sausage
- · 8 oz. cream cheese
- · 1 (4 oz.) can mushrooms
- · Dash of Worcestershire
- · Dash of crushed red pepper – more if you like it spicy

Cook sausage until brown—drain; add mushrooms and let mixture simmer. Cut cream cheese into small cubes and add to sausage/mushroom mixture. Stir until melted. Add Worcestershire and crushed red pepper. Let simmer.

Serve hot with corn chips.

Point of Grace's Garden Party Fondue

· 1 small onion, diced
· ¼ c. butter
· 2 (8 oz.) packages cream cheese
· ¼ c. milk
· ¼ c. Parmesan cheese
· 1 small jar dried beef, diced
· Raw veggies, tortilla chips, or crackers for dipping

Sauté chopped onion in butter. Over medium to low heat slowly melt in cream cheese, milk, Parmesan cheese, and dried beef. Heat until smooth and warm.

Serve warm with raw vegetables, chips, or crackers.

The Mont's Hot Bean Dip

· 2 (16 oz.) cans of refried beans
· 2 Tbsp. bacon drippings
· 7 oz. hot sauce
· 5 Tbsp. onion, diced
· 3 - 4 oz. beer
· 1 tsp. cumin
· 2 tsp. garlic salt
· 1 tsp. cayenne pepper
· 4 Tbsp. diced jalapeños

Warm the beans in a double boiler or over very low heat. Sauté onion and hot sauce in the bacon drippings, then add the beer. Simmer for 3 to 4 minutes over medium heat until the color changes. Add spices and jalapeños while simmering. Mix all ingredients in the double boiler with the beans and stir well.

Serve hot with warm chips and extra hot sauce (recipe below).

Easy Hot Sauce
· I (24 oz.) can of stewed tomatoes
· 5 oz. pickled jalapeños
· ½ c. red onion, diced

Mix ingredients in blender to desired consistency.

Cheese Sauce

· 3 Tbsp. butter
· 3 Tbsp. flour
· 1 c. milk
· ½ small onion, finely chopped
· ½ c. Parmesan cheese

Melt butter over low heat. Add flour, stirring until blended and smooth. Add milk, slowly stirring constantly. Add onion and cheese. Cook until thickened.

Good sauce for chicken or vegetables.

Yields about 1 ¼ cups

Edamame Purée

· 2 c. shelled frozen edamame
· 1 shallot, peeled and roughly chopped
· 1 Tbsp. olive oil
· ¼ tsp. kosher salt
· ¼ tsp. white pepper or freshly ground black pepper

Add edamame and shallot to 4 cups boiling water, boiling for 5 to 6 minutes. Drain, reserving the cooking liquid.

Place the edamame and ¼ cup of the cooking liquid in a food processor, along with the oil, salt and pepper. Puree until smooth. Add more cooking liquid for a lighter puree.

Serve as a dip with crostinis or as a topping for grilled fish.

"Chic" Fried Chickpeas

· 2 cans garbanzo beans
· 1 ½ c. olive oil
· 2 Tbsp. sea salt
· 3 Tbsp. crushed rosemary

Preheat oven to 200°.

Rinse and drain garbanzo beans. Spread beans onto several layers of paper towels and gently rub to loosen skins.

Heat olive oil in a deep saucepan on medium-high. Fry beans in batches, stirring frequently (about 10 minutes) until firm. Test by removing a bean and breaking it open. It should be fried completely through without soft spots, turning a golden brown. Drain beans, place in an ovenproof dish, and put in oven. Fry remaining batches.

Toss with crushed rosemary and sea salt. Store in airtight container.

Marinated Olives

· 2 c. large green olives
· 1 lemon, zested
· 1 Tbsp. fresh rosemary, stripped from stem
· 1 Tbsp. fresh thyme, stripped from stem
· 1 Tbsp. fresh basil, torn
· 1 tsp. sea salt
· ½ tsp. freshly ground black pepper
· Extra-virgin olive oil

Pour olives in a shallow bowl; add lemon zest and herbs and season with salt and pepper. Toss gently and cover with olive oil. The longer it marinates, the better it tastes.

4-Bit Goodies

· 1 (8 oz.) package cream cheese, softened
· 3 tsp. onion, grated
· 1 c. mayonnaise
· ½ tsp. cayenne pepper
· ½ c. Parmesan cheese
· 4 Tbsp. chives
· Bread – white, wheat, rye, pumpernickel, or your favorite

Preheat oven to 350°.

Mix first six ingredients well. Cut bread with 1½-inch round cookie cutter. Spread cheese mixture on each piece of bread and place on ungreased cookie sheet.

Bake at 350° for 10 to 15 minutes or until cheese topping is bubbly hot.

Note – To prepare in advance, quick freeze on a cookie sheet. Place in a freezer bag to store frozen. To cook, take out desired number and bake.

Also great with soups and salads!

Makes about 6 dozen.

Stuffed Mushrooms

· 2 lbs. fresh whole mushrooms
· 8 oz. cream cheese, softened
· 1 lb. bacon, cooked and crumbled
· 4 green onions, chopped fine
· 2 c. shredded Colby cheese
· ⅓ c. butter

Remove stems from mushrooms and discard.

Mix together cream cheese, bacon, shredded cheese, and green onions and stuff into mushrooms. Place in a baking dish. Dot tops of mushrooms with butter.

Bake at 350° for 20 minutes; serve hot.

Aunt Phil's Healthy Snack

· 2 packages Ramen noodles – you will
   not use flavor packets
· 1 c. sunflower seeds
· 1 c. slivered almonds

Preheat oven to 350°.

Crunch noodles and mix with other ingredients. Spread on cookie sheet.

Bake at 350° for 10 minutes.

Spicy Pretzels

· 1 (1 lb.) bag of pretzels
· 1 packet of powdered ranch dip mix
· 1 tsp. Cayenne pepper
· 1 tsp. garlic powder
· ⅓ c. vegetable oil

Preheat oven to 250°.

Mix spices together, then whisk in oil. Toss pretzels to coat.

Spread on baking sheet and bake for 20 minutes at 250°.

Bread

Beer Bread

· 3 c. self-rising flour
· ½ c. sugar
· 1 bottle warm beer or large can
· ½ stick butter, melted

Preheat oven to 350°.

Mix all ingredients together, except butter. Pour into a loaf pan and bake for 45 minutes at 350°. Remove from oven and pour melted butter over the top. Bake for 15 more minutes.

Coolrise Honey Lemon Whole Wheat Bread

· 3 ¼ - 4 ¼ c. all-purpose flour
· 2 packages dry yeast
· 1 tsp. salt
· ¼ c. honey
· 3 Tbsp. margarine, softened
· 1 Tbsp. grated lemon peel
· 2 ¼ c. hot tap water
· 2 c. whole wheat flour
· Salad oil
· Melted butter, for brushing

Combine 2 cups all-purpose flour, dissolved yeast, and salt in a large bowl. Add honey, margarine, and lemon peel. Add hot tap water all at once. Beat with mixer at medium speed for 2 minutes, scraping bowl occasionally. Add 1 cup whole wheat flour. Beat at high speed for 1 minute, scraping bowl occasionally. Stir in remaining cup whole wheat flour with wooden spoon. Gradually stir in just enough remaining all-purpose flour to make a soft dough.

Knead 5 to 10 minutes, until dough is smooth and elastic. Cover with plastic wrap, then with a towel. Let rest 20 minutes, and then punch down. Divide dough into 2 parts, and roll each part into an 8×12-inch rectangle. Roll up tightly into loaves, beginning at 8-inch side. Seal lengthwise and press ends.

Place in greased 8 ½×4 ½×2 ½-inch pan. Brush surface with oil. Cover pans loosely with waxed paper, then with plastic wrap. Refrigerate 2 to 24 hours.

When ready to bake, uncover and let stand for 10 minutes. Bake at 400° for 35 to 40 minutes. Remove from pans immediately. Brush surface with melted butter.

Pull-Apart Bread

· 1 c. milk
· ¾ c. butter
· 1 ½ tsp. salt
· ½ c. sugar
· 1 package dry yeast
· ¼ c. warm water
· 1 tsp. sugar
· 3 eggs
· 4 c. sifted flour
· 1 c. melted butter
· Sesame seeds

Scald 1 cup milk, add ¾ cup butter, 1 ½ teaspoons salt, and ½ cup sugar. Let cool.

Add 1 dry yeast package which has been dissolved in ¼ cup lukewarm water with 1 teaspoon sugar until bubbly.

Add 3 eggs that have been beaten with a fork until foamy. Then add 4 cups of sifted flour. Cover and let stand until it rises to double in size. Stir down and refrigerate overnight.

Next morning: Grease 3 cake pans (8-inch), melt 2 cubes butter. Take ⅓ of dough out of the refrigerator leaving remainder in refrigerator. Place dough on lightly floured wax paper. Pat out to be 6 inches wide and ½-inch thick. Cut in strips with a knife, dipping it in flour. Cut strips ½-wide. Strips are about 6 × ½ × ½-inch. Begin in the middle of the cake pan and go around, dipping each strip in the pan of melted butter. Where each strip ends dip another strip in melted butter and start there. Do not place strips jammed up together, nor fill the pan too full. Adjust if necessary. Pat the top of dough down pressing ends together if separated. Sprinkle the top with sesame seeds and let rise until double in size, about 1 ½ hours in a warm place.

Bake the 3 pans at 350° for 15 minutes. The dough will come up to the top of the pan. Cool. Wrap in foil and freeze.

When ready to serve the bread, take out of the freezer, place on folded foil, bake 15 more minutes at 350°. Cover (brush) with ½ cube of melted butter (½ cube for each pan of bread) and push off onto your serving dish.

Serve with jelly or preserves.

Note – Variations with dough: Dinner rolls freeze beautifully. Makes cinnamon rolls, orange rolls, or coffee cakes.

Onion-Cheese Bread

· 1 Tbsp. vegetable oil
· ¾ c. finely diced onion
· ½ c. milk
· 1 egg, beaten
· 1 ½ c. Bisquick®
· 1 c. shredded cheddar cheese, divided
· ½ tsp. onion salt
· 2 Tbsp. melted butter
· 1 Tbsp. chopped chives

Preheat oven to 400°.

In a small skillet, heat the oil; sauté onion until tender.

Combine milk, egg, and Bisquick®. Add sautéed onion and ½ cup of the cheese. Stir until moistened. Spread the dough into a greased 8-inch round pan.

Stir the onion salt into the melted butter. Drizzle over the dough and sprinkle with chives.

Bake at 400° for 15 minutes. Remove from oven and sprinkle with remaining ½ cup cheese. Return to the oven and bake 5 more minutes or until golden brown. Cut into wedges and serve warm.

Simple Yeast Bread

· 4 c. lukewarm water
· 6 c. flour
· 1 ½ Tbsp. dry yeast
· 1 ½ Tbsp. kosher salt

Mix: In a large container, mix all ingredients. Put a lid on container, but leave it slightly open. Let sit for 2 hours on the counter, then put in fridge for up to 14 days.

Bake: Preheat oven to 450° and place a 9×13-inch glass or metal pan in the oven while it is warming – it will later be filled with water to make steam.

With floured hands, take a softball sized lump of dough and place on a cookie sheet that has been coated in cornmeal or cooking spray. Let sit about 20 minutes to rise, then make 3 slashes across the top before baking.

Pour 2 cups of water into the hot pan in the oven. Bake bread for 25 to 35 minutes or until browned.

Whole Wheat and Rosemary Focaccia

· 1 c. warm water
· 1 Tbsp. sugar
· 1 ¼ oz. envelope dry yeast

In a large bowl, combine water and sugar. Sprinkle with dry yeast. Let stand 5 minutes.

· 2 Tbsp. olive oil
· 2 c. all-purpose flour
· ½ c. whole wheat flour
· 1 tsp. salt

Stir in olive oil, flour, and salt. Mix well. Add more flour if needed to make soft dough. Knead dough until soft and smooth, about 8 minutes. Grease a large bowl and add the dough. Cover and let stand at room temperature until dough doubles in size – takes about 1 hour.

· 1 Tbsp. olive oil
· 1 Tbsp. fresh or ½ Tbsp. dried rosemary
· 1 garlic clove, finely chopped

Heat oil, rosemary, and garlic until it sizzles. Remove from heat to let cool.

Preheat oven to 400°.

When dough is ready, punch down and place in center of nonstick baking sheet. Stretch to 12-inch circle. Brush with cooled rosemary oil.

Bake at 400° on bottom oven rack until brown and crispy, 12 to 20 minutes. Cool then slice into 2-inch squares.

Quick Tomato and Garlic Focaccia

· 10 oz. package refrigerated pizza crust dough
· 2 Tbsp. olive oil
· 3 garlic cloves, finely minced
· ⅓ c. crumbled Feta (optional)
· ½ c. thinly sliced tomato
· Coarse salt

Preheat oven to 400°.

Unroll the dough into an ungreased baking sheet with a rim. Stretch the dough into a rectangle. Make indentations in the dough with your fingertips. Drizzle the olive oil over the dough. Scatter the garlic and Feta (if using) over the dough. Arrange the tomato slices evenly over the dough. Sprinkle the coarse salt over the top.

Bake until golden brown, 15 to 18 minutes. Cool slightly, just until able to handle. Slice into squares.

Rosemary Bread-Machine Bread

· 1 ½ c. water, 80-90° F
· 4 Tbsp. extra-virgin olive oil
· 1 ½ tsp. sea salt
· 4 c. bread flour
· 4 tsp. dried rosemary
· 2 ¼ tsp. active dry yeast

Place ingredients, in the order listed, in the bread pan
fitted with the kneading paddle. Place the bread pan in the
bread maker. Choose the white bread setting, crust size
large and press start.

Breakfast

Low-Fat Banana Nut Muffins

· 1 ½ c. all-purpose flour
· 1 tsp. baking powder
· 1 tsp. baking soda
· ½ tsp. salt
· 1 tsp. cinnamon
· 3 large very ripe bananas, mashed
· ¾ c. white sugar
· 1 egg
· 1 tsp. vanilla
· ⅓ c. applesauce
· ½ - 1 c. walnuts (optional)

Preheat oven to 350°.

Coat muffin pans with non-stick spray, or use paper liners. Whisk together flour, baking powder, baking soda, salt, and cinnamon; set aside.

Combine bananas, sugar, egg, vanilla, and applesauce, and mix until smooth. Mix into dry ingredients. Fold in walnuts. Scoop batter into muffin pans.

Bake mini muffins for 10 to 15 minutes and large muffins for 25 to 30 minutes. Muffins will spring back when lightly tapped.

Sausage Brunch Mini Muffins

· 1 lb. ground sausage
· 3 c. Bisquick®
· 1 ½ c. shredded cheddar cheese
· 1 can cream soup (Cream of Onion
    or Cream of Mushroom)
· ¾ - 1 c. water
· 3 - 4 drops of Tabasco® (optional)
· 1 Tbsp. dried parsley flakes

Preheat oven to 375°.

Brown sausage and drain on paper towels. Combine sausage, Bisquick®, and cheese. Mix soup and water and add to sausage mixture. Add Tabasco® and parsley, to taste. Spoon mixture into mini muffin pans, filling each cup to the top.

Bake at 375° for 20 to 25 minutes, or until golden brown. Allow to rest briefly, and then remove to cool on racks.

Note – Can be frozen and thawed when needed.

Makes approximately 36 mini muffins.

Spicy Bran Muffins

- ⅔ c. unsifted all-purpose flour
- 2 Tbsp. sugar
- 2 ½ tsp. baking powder
- 1 tsp. cinnamon
- ⅛ tsp. allspice
- ⅛ tsp. cloves
- ¼ tsp. salt
- 1 egg, beaten
- ¾ c. milk
- 3 Tbsp. shortening, melted
- 1 ½ c. Raisin Bran cereal

Preheat oven to 425°.

Mix together flour, sugar, baking powder, spices, and salt.

Combine egg and milk; add to flour mixture. Then add shortening and mix only enough to moisten flour. Fold in cereal.

Fill greased muffin pans ⅔ full. Bake at 425° for 15 to 20 minutes, or until golden brown.

Makes 8 medium muffins.

Glazed Lemon Nut Bread

- ¼ c. butter or margarine, softened
- ¾ c. sugar
- 2 eggs
- 2 c. all-purpose flour
- 2 ½ tsp. baking powder
- 1 tsp. salt
- ¾ c. milk
- 2 tsp. grated lemon rind
- ½ c. walnuts, finely chopped
- ¼ c. plus 1 Tbsp. sifted confectioners' sugar
- 1 tsp. lemon juice

Preheat oven to 350°.

Cream butter; gradually add ¾ cup sugar, beating until light and fluffy. Add eggs, one at a time, beating well after each addition.

Combine flour, baking powder, and salt; add to creamed mixture alternately with milk, beginning and ending with flour mixture. Stir in lemon rind and walnuts. Pour batter into a greased 9×5×3-inch loaf pan.

Bake at 350° for 45 to 50 minutes; remove to a wire rack and let cool completely.

Combine confectioners' sugar and lemon juice; stir until smooth. Drizzle glaze over top of bread.

Makes 1 loaf.

Cream Cheese Braid

Pastry
· 1 c. sour cream
· ½ c. sugar
· 1 tsp. salt
· ½ c. melted margarine
· ½ c. warm water
· 2 packages dry yeast
· 2 eggs, beaten
· 4 c. flour

Filling
· 16 oz. cream cheese, softened
· ¾ c. sugar
· 1 egg, beaten
· ⅛ tsp. salt
· 2 tsp. vanilla

Glaze
· 2 c. confectioners' sugar
· 4 Tbsp. milk
· 2 tsp. vanilla

On the first day: Heat sour cream over low heat. Stir in sugar, salt, and margarine. Cool to lukewarm. Dissolve yeast in warm water. Combine sour cream mixture, yeast mixture, eggs and flour. Mix well; cover and refrigerate overnight.

On the next day: Combine cream cheese and sugar. Then add egg, salt, and vanilla.

Preheat oven to 375°.

Divide dough into fourths. Roll one of the fourths into a 12×8-inch rectangle. Spread ¼ of the cream cheese filling over this dough. Roll up jelly roll-style, pinching the edges to seal it. Place seam-side down on a greased baking sheet and make slits ⅔ of the way down at 2-inch intervals to resemble braids. Cover and let rise till double (approximately 1 hour). Bake at 375° for 12 to 15 minutes.

Pour glaze over braid while warm.

Serves 6-8 per braid. Recipe yields 4 braids.

Philadelphia Cinnamon Buns

· 1 package yeast
· ¼ c. warm water
· 1 ¼ c. milk, scalded
· 1 ½ tsp. salt
· 5 c. flour
· 1 Tbsp. sugar
· ½ c. shortening
· ¾ c. sugar
· 2 eggs
· Butter or margarine
· Light corn syrup
· Brown sugar
· Cinnamon
· Raisins and/or chopped pecans (optional)

Put ¼ cup warm water in a cup and sprinkle in 1 package granulated yeast and 1 Tbsp. sugar. Cover and let stand 5 minutes.

Scald milk and cool till lukewarm. Add salt to yeast mixture, and stir until smooth. Stir in milk.

Pour 2 cups of flour in a bowl; make a well in the flour, pour in milk mixture; beat until light, cover and set aside.

Beat ½ cup shortening until light. Gradually beat in ¾ cup sugar, then the eggs, one at a time. When the yeast mixture looks light and bubbly, add the shortening, sugar, and egg mixture a big spoonful at a time, beating it in. When well beaten, STIR in 3 more cups flour, a small amount at a time, mixing well. Cover and let rise in warm place until double in bulk.

Preheat oven to 350°.

Take a third of the dough at a time; roll out on floured surface about ¼-inch thick. Spread with softened butter, sprinkle with brown sugar and cinnamon and raisins, if you like. Trickle light corn syrup over all, then roll it up and cut into 1-inch slices. Place in 8 or 9-inch round pans that have been prepared with melted butter and corn syrup. (If desired, sprinkle some chopped pecans or raisins in the pans.) Cover and let rise until doubled in bulk.

Bake at 350° until brown, about 30 minutes. When done, turn from pans at once.

Sour Cream Coffee Cake

Cake
· ½ lb. margarine
· 2 c. sugar
· 1 pt. sour cream
· 4 eggs
· 4 c. flour
· 2 tsp. baking soda
· 2 tsp. baking powder
· 2 tsp. vanilla

Topping
· 1 c. brown sugar
· 2 - 4 Tbsp. cinnamon
· ½ c. chopped walnuts

Preheat oven to 350°.

Mix all cake ingredients together. Mix all topping ingredients together. Put cake and topping in alternate layers in an angel food pan which has been greased and floured.

Bake at 350° for 1 hour and 15 minutes. Do not open door until time is up. Do not invert pan. Cool 15 minutes. Turn out of pan.

Serves 16 - 20.

Poppyseed Teacakes

· 3 eggs
· 1 ½ c. milk
· 1 ½ c. oil
· 1 ½ tsp. vanilla
· 1 ½ tsp. butter flavoring
· 1 ½ tsp. almond flavoring
· 1 ½ tsp. salt
· 1 ½ tsp. baking powder
· 3 c. flour
· 2 c. sugar
· 1 ½ Tbsp. poppyseeds

Preheat oven to 350°.

Use a mixer to combine first six ingredients. Combine remaining ingredients and add to first mixture. Mix well. Pour batter into greased mini-muffin tins.

Bake 15 to 20 minutes or until done.

Variation:
To make a loaf cake, pour batter into greased loaf pan and bake for 1 hour at 350°.

Oatmeal Bread

· 2 c. boiling water
· 1 c. oats
· ½ c. sorghum molasses
· 2 Tbsp. Crisco®
· 2 tsp. salt
· 1 envelope active dry yeast
· ½ c. lukewarm water
· 6 c. unsifted flour

Pour boiling water over oats, molasses, Crisco®, and salt. Cool to lukewarm.

Dissolve yeast in ½ cup lukewarm water and add to first mixture. Beat in all of the flour and knead until smooth. Place in greased bowl, cover, and let rise for 1 hour.

Divide dough in half, shape loaves, and place in greased loaf pans. Let rise until doubled in bulk.

Bake at 325° for 1 hour.

Makes 2 loaves.

Note – A delicious health bread can be made by substituting 1 cup Miller's Bran for 1 cup flour making 5 cups of flour, 1 cup bran, and 1 cup oats.

Pancake Puff

· ½ c. all-purpose flour
· ½ tsp. salt
· ½ c. milk
· 3 eggs

Preheat oven to 400°.

Lightly grease 6 custard cups. Mix all ingredients and pour into cups.

Bake at 400° for 20 minutes or until golden.

Turn out of custard cups onto dish. Serve with syrup or fruit.

Pumpkin Pancakes with Yogurt Raisin Topping

Topping
· 2 c. low-fat vanilla yogurt
· 1 c. raisins

Pancakes
· 1 c. all-purpose flour
· 1 Tbsp. sugar
· 2 tsp. baking powder
· ½ tsp. cinnamon
· 1 c. 1% low fat milk
· 2 Tbsp. melted butter
· 1 egg
· ½ c. canned pumpkin
· ½ c. low-fat vanilla yogurt

Topping: In a small mixing bowl, combine 2 cups vanilla yogurt and raisins. Reserve.

To make the pancakes: combine flour, sugar, baking powder, and cinnamon in a large mixing bowl.

In a medium mixing bowl, combine milk, butter, egg, pumpkin, and ½ cup yogurt, mixing well. Add wet ingredients to flour mixture and stir until just moist. Do not overmix. Batter may be lumpy. For thinner batter, add milk.

Lightly coat a griddle or skillet with cooking spray and heat on medium. Using a quarter-cup measure, pour batter onto hot griddle. Cook until bubbles begin to burst then flip pancakes and cook until golden. Serve warm, topped with yogurt-raisin mixture and dusting of cinnamon.

Makes 12 pancakes, or 4 servings.

Breakfast Fruit Salad

· 1 c. red or green grapes, halved
· 1 c. coconut
· 1 c. pineapple tidbits, drained
· 1 c. mandarin oranges, halved
· 1 c. mini marshmallows
· ½ c. maraschino cherries, halved
· ½ c. pecans, finely chopped
· 1 c. yogurt or light sour cream (yogurt flavor of your choice)
· 2 sliced bananas

Combine all ingredients well, except bananas. Mix and refrigerate at least 1 hour.

Add banana slices just before serving and mix well. Bite size pieces of fruit work best.

Brunch Casserole

· 1 lb. ground sausage
· 1 (8 oz.) can crescent dinner rolls
· 2 c. shredded Mozzarella cheese
· 4 eggs, beaten
· ¾ c. milk
· ¼ tsp. salt
· ⅛ tsp. pepper

Preheat oven to 425°.

Crumble sausage in skillet and brown over medium heat until cooked. Drain.

Line bottom of a 9×13×2-inch glass baking dish with rolls, firmly pressing perforations in rolls to seal. Sprinkle rolls with sausage and cheese.

Combine remaining ingredients. Beat well and pour over sausage.

Bake at 425° for 15 to 20 minutes or until set. Let stand 5 minutes. Cut into squares and serve immediately.

Easy Green Chile Breakfast Casserole

· 1 - 1 ½ lbs. ground sausage
· 1 lb. grated aged cheddar cheese
· 2 (4 oz.) cans chopped green chiles
· 8 eggs
· Salt and pepper, to taste

Preheat oven to 350°.

Crumble sausage in a skillet and brown, drain well.

Drain can of chiles, reserving the liquid. Whisk together the eggs and the reserved chile liquid. Add salt and pepper to taste.

Spray casserole dish with cooking spray. Layer ingredients in the following order: 1st – green chiles, 2nd – sausage, 3rd – cheese, then repeat layers. Pour egg mixture over the top of casserole.

Bake at 350° for approximately 45 minutes. Depending on number of eggs and dish depth, could be 30 to 60 minutes.

Note – Recipe can easily be doubled for large group, or cut in half, if needed.

Eggs Florentine Casserole

· 1 (10 oz.) package frozen spinach
· 2 c. shredded Swiss cheese, divided
· 1 lb. ground sausage
· 2 c. sliced fresh mushrooms
· 6 green onions, chopped
· 2 Tbsp. butter or margarine, melted
· 12 large eggs, lightly beaten
· 2 c. whipping cream
· ¼ tsp. paprika

Preheat oven to 350°.

Cook spinach according to package directions, drain well.

Sprinkle 1 cup of cheese in the bottom of lightly greased 9×13-inch baking dish. Spread spinach over cheese.

Brown sausage in skillet, stirring until it crumbles. Drain and sprinkle over spinach.

Sauté mushrooms and green onion in butter over medium heat until tender. Sprinkle sautéed vegetables over sausage.

Combine eggs and cream, beating with a whisk until blended. Pour egg mixture over vegetable mixture. Top with remaining cheese and sprinkle with paprika.

Bake, uncovered, at 350° for 40 minutes or until set.

Family French Toast

· 1 c. light brown sugar
· ½ c. melted butter, cooled
· 2 Tbsp. light corn syrup
· 1 large loaf Italian or French bread
· 6 eggs
· 2 c. milk
· 1 ½ tsp. vanilla
· ¼ tsp. cinnamon
· Dash of nutmeg

Combine sugar, butter, and corn syrup. Pour into and 9×13-inch baking dish.

Slice bread to ½-inch thickness. Place on sugar mixture.

Beat eggs, milk, and vanilla. Pour over bread. Sprinkle with cinnamon and nutmeg.

Cover and refrigerate overnight.

Bake at 325° for 30 to 35 minutes.

Serve with maple syrup.

Steve Owens' Sausage Egg Casserole

· 1 lb. sausage
· 6 eggs
· 2 c. milk
· 1 tsp. salt
· 1 tsp. dry mustard
· 6 slices bread (broken into pieces)
· 1 ½ c. shredded cheddar cheese
· 1 (4 oz.) can mushroom pieces

Brown sausage and drain. Set aside.

Beat eggs and milk. Add salt and dry mustard. Beat again.

Add bread pieces and stir in cheddar cheese, sausage, and mushrooms. Pour into greased 9×13-inch pan.

Refrigerate overnight.

Bake uncovered at 350° for 40 to 45 minutes. Let stand a few minutes before serving.

Serves 8.

Healthy Granola

Dry ingredients
· 6 c. rolled oats
· 2 c. raw almonds or pecan halves, or a mixture
· ¾ c. sesame seeds
· ¾ c. light brown sugar
· 2 tsp. ground cinnamon
· 1 tsp. ground ginger
· 1 tsp. salt

Wet ingredients
· 1 c. unsweetened apple sauce
· ¼ c. honey
· 2 Tbsp. Olive Oil

Set racks in the upper and lower thirds of the oven. Preheat the oven to 300°. In a large bowl, combine all of the dry ingredients. Stir to mix well.

In a small bowl, combine all of the wet ingredients. Stir to mix well.

Pour the wet ingredients over the dry ones, and stir well. Spread the mixture evenly on 2 rimmed baking sheets. Bake for 35 to 40 minutes, or until evenly golden brown. Set a timer to go off every 10 minutes while the granola bakes, so you can rotate the pans and give the granola a good stir; this helps it to cook evenly.

Remove the pans from the oven, stir well – this will keep it from cooling into a hard, solid sheet – and set aside to cool. The finished granola may still feel slightly soft when it comes out of the oven, but it will crisp as it cools. Scoop cooled granola into to a large zipper-lock plastic bag or other airtight container. Store in the refrigerator.

Yield: about 10 cups

Lighter Fare

Interurban's Urban Sandwich

· 6-inch cracked wheat bun
· Butter, for bread
· 2 oz. turkey, thinly sliced
· 2 oz. ham, thinly sliced
· 2 oz. pastrami, thinly sliced
· 2 Italian salad peppers, or pepperoncini
· 1 leaf of green or red leaf lettuce
· 1 slice Provolone cheese
· 1 slice Swiss cheese
· 1 tomato, sliced
· Sprinkle of oregano, to taste
· Onion slices and pickles, for garnish

Slice bun lengthwise and butter. Spread each meat evenly on bottom of bun. Slice cheese slices in half and place on top of meats. Place leaf lettuce on top of cheese, tomato slices on top of lettuce, and peppers on top of tomatoes. Whole salad peppers should be sliced on one side and opened to get maximum coverage. Sprinkle with oregano, and place top of bun on sandwich.

Slice sandwich diagonally and place frilled toothpick in each half. Separate halves on plate for visual appeal and garnish plate with onion slice and pickle.

Grilled Chicken Caprese Sandwich

· 4 mini ciabatta loaves
· 2 tomatoes, sliced
· 8 slices fresh Mozzarella cheese
· Fresh snipped basil
· Extra-virgin olive oil
· Salt and pepper to taste
· 2 Tbsp. balsamic vinegar
· 1 garlic clove, minced
· 1 Tbsp. poultry seasoning
· 4 boneless, skinless chicken breasts

Season chicken with poultry seasoning and garlic. Grill chicken on indoor or outdoor grill or grill pan until cooked. Allow to rest for 10 minutes, and then slice cooked chicken.

Sprinkle ciabatta bread with olive oil, and grill bread until warm with grill marks. Top each ciabatta loaf with sliced chicken, 2 slices of tomatoes, 2 slices of fresh Mozzarella, fresh snipped basil, olive oil, and balsamic vinegar. Season with salt and pepper to taste.

Italian Pub Burgers

· 2 cloves garlic, peeled
· ½ c. packed fresh flat-leaf parsley
· 2 ¼ lbs. 80/20 ground beef or ground chuck
· ¾ c. grated Parmesan cheese
· 3 Tbsp. tomato paste
· 1 ¾ tsp. kosher salt
· ¼ tsp. freshly ground black pepper
· 9 small ciabatta rolls, sliced in half
· ¼ c. extra-virgin olive oil
· 9 slices Fontina or Havarti cheese
· 9 large basil leaves

Place a grill pan over medium-high heat, or preheat a gas or charcoal grill.

Place the garlic and parsley in the bowl of a food processor, and pulse until finely chopped. Add the ground beef, Parmesan cheese, tomato paste, salt, and pepper. Pulse until ingredients are combined. Form the mixture into 9 patties.

Place burgers on the grill and cook for 4 to 5 minutes on each side. Brush the cut side of each roll with the olive oil and toast on the grill for 1 to 2 minutes until slightly golden.

To serve, place 1 mini burger on the bottom half of each of the rolls. Place 1 slice of Fontina or Havarti cheese on top of the burgers. Place the basil leaf on top of the cheese and cover with the top half of the bun.

Southwest Chicken Salad Sandwiches

· 1 whole rotisserie chicken, pulled
· 1 red bell pepper, diced
· 2 whole jalapeños
· 3 Tbsp. olive oil
· 1 bunch cilantro
· ½ can black beans
· ½ can corn
· 1 c. light Miracle Whip® or mayonnaise
· Cumin, to taste
· Garlic salt, to taste
· Salt and pepper, to taste

In a large mixing bowl, combine the Miracle Whip® or mayonnaise, pulled chicken, half of the red pepper, black beans, and corn.

In a food processor or blender, mix cilantro, jalapeños, and other half of red pepper with cumin, garlic salt, and salt and pepper to taste. Mix until it is a puree consistency. Combine all ingredients and chill in refrigerator.

Serve on bread or rolls.

Legend's Spinach Quiche

· 1 baked pie shell
· 3 oz. thinly sliced ham or 3 oz. cooked bacon
· 3 oz. grated Swiss cheese
· 3 whole eggs
· ¼ tsp. salt
· ½ tsp. pepper
· ½ tsp. nutmeg
· ¼ tsp. garlic powder
· 1 c. scalded cream
· 1 package chopped spinach, cooked
· 2 Tbsp. bacon fat

Preheat oven to 350°.

Cook spinach, drain, and mix with bacon fat. Mix all other ingredients and then add spinach. Put whole mixture in the baked pie shell.

Bake at 350° in regular oven until knife, when inserted in center of pie, comes out clean.

Photo provided by Legend's

Quiche

· 2 deep-dish pie crusts
· Enough mushrooms and onions to fill
    bottom of both pie crusts
· Butter, to sauté vegetables
· Ham
· 1 lb. bacon, cooked and drained
· 1 box frozen broccoli, chopped
· 6 eggs
· 2 c. half and half
· ¼ tsp. dried mustard
· 4 (6 oz.) packages of Swiss or Mozzarella
    cheese, cut in slices
· Paprika

Preheat oven to 375°.

Prepare pie crust according to package directions.

Fry bacon and drain. Sauté mushrooms and onions together in butter.

Mix eggs, half and half, and mustard together and set aside.

Spread mushrooms and onions on bottom of pie shells. Next, layer ham, bacon, broccoli, and cheese until you have used all — the last layer is cheese. Pour egg mixture over all. Sprinkle paprika on top.

Bake at 375° until brown on top, about 40 minutes.

Each quiche serves 4.

Salad with Blueberry Vinaigrette

Salad
· 2 bunches leaf spinach or other greens
· 1 pt. fresh blueberries
· Sliced strawberries
· ⅔ c. bleu cheese or Feta
· ½ c. sugared pecans (recipe below)

Toss salad ingredients together in large bowl.

Blueberry Vinaigrette
· 1 shallot, minced
· ½ pt. fresh blueberries
· 1 tsp. salt
· 3 Tbsp. sugar
· ⅓ c. raspberry vinegar
· 1 c. vegetable or canola oil

Combine shallot, berries, salt, sugar, vinegar and oil in a blender until smooth. Toss with salad just before serving.

Sugared Pecans
· 1 egg white
· 1 Tbsp. water
· 1 lb. pecan halves
· 1 c. sugar
· ¾ tsp. salt
· ½ tsp. cinnamon

Preheat oven to 250°.

Grease a baking sheet. Whip egg white with water until frothy.

In another bowl, combine sugar, salt, and cinnamon.

Add pecans to egg; stir to coat. Remove, then toss in sugar mixture until coated. Spread on baking sheet. Bake for 1 hour, stirring every 15 minutes.

Legend's Poppyseed Dressing

· 1 ½ c. sugar
· 2 tsp. salt
· 2 tsp. dry mustard
· ⅔ c. white vinegar
· 3 tsp. onion juice (optional)
· 2 c. peanut oil
· 3 Tbsp. poppyseeds

Mix sugar, salt, mustard, and vinegar. Add onion juice, if using, and stir in thoroughly. Add oil slowly and beat constantly until thick. Add poppyseeds and beat until distributed. Keep refrigerated.

Buttery Garlic Croutons

· 1 baguette
· ½ c. butter, melted
· 1 tsp. olive oil
· 2 - 3 garlic cloves, crushed
· Sea salt, to taste
· Freshly cracked pepper, to taste
· Add additional herbs, including, basil, thyme, rosemary, etc. to your preference

Preheat oven to 350°.

Cut bread into medium cubes. Combine melted butter, olive oil, garlic, salt, and pepper. Drizzle on bread cubes. Mix well and place on foil-covered cooking sheet.

Bake at 350° for 30 minutes. Turn oven off and leave bread in oven until cool. Place in plastic zip bag.

Mediterranean Summer Salad

· 8 oz. orzo pasta
· 2 c. cherry tomatoes, halved
· 1 c. fresh basil leaves, chopped
· 1 tsp. garlic, minced
· ¼ c. pine nuts, toasted
· ½ c. kalamata olives, pitted and halved
· 4 oz. Feta cheese, broken into large chunks
· 2 c. fresh baby spinach leaves
· 1 Tbsp. extra-virgin olive oil
· 2 Tbsp. balsamic vinegar
· Salt and freshly ground black pepper, to taste

Cook orzo according to package directions.

Meanwhile, in a large bowl, combine tomatoes, basil, garlic, pine nuts, olives, Feta, and spinach. Add cooked and cooled orzo.

In a small bowl, whisk together oil, vinegar, salt and pepper to taste, and toss with salad.

Bleu Cheese Salad and Dressing

· ¼ c. olive oil
· ¼ c. canola or safflower oil
· ¼ c. white wine vinegar
· 1 tsp. salt and pepper, to taste
· 1 medium onion, thinly sliced in rings
· ½ small head cauliflower (3 c.)
· ½ c. sliced radishes
· ½ c. crumbled bleu cheese
· Romaine and iceberg lettuce

Combine oils, vinegar, salt, pepper, and sliced vegetables. Marinate 30 minutes.

Tear lettuce, place in bowls, add cheese, then pour on dressing and toss.

Serves 4-6.

Chopped Salad with Homemade Red Wine Vinaigrette

· 4 scallions
· 1 cucumber
· 1 handful fresh basil
· 1 head butter lettuce
· 2 bunches romaine lettuce
· 1 c. shredded carrots
· 10 grape tomatoes, cut into halves or quarters
· Pine nuts (toasted)
· Parmesan cheese

Slice vegetables into equal-size pieces. Add to a bowl and make the dressing below and toss until coated. Plate the salad and top with grated Parmesan cheese and toasted pine nuts.

Red Wine Vinaigrette Dressing

· 2 Tbsp. extra-virgin olive oil
· 1 Tbsp. red wine vinegar
· 1 tsp. Dijon mustard
· Salt and pepper, to taste

In a small bowl, mix Dijon mustard, oil, and vinegar. Whisk and add salt and pepper.

Serves 4-6.

Indian Spinach Salad

· ¼ c. white wine vinegar
· ¼ c. olive oil
· 2 Tbsp. mango chutney, chopped
· 2 tsp. sugar
· ½ tsp. salt
· 1 ½ tsp. curry powder
· 1 tsp. dry mustard
· 8 c. fresh spinach, torn in bite-size pieces
· 1 ½ c. apples, chopped
· ½ c. light raisins
· ½ c. peanuts
· 2 Tbsp. green onion, sliced

In a jar, combine vinegar, oil, chutney, sugar, salt, curry powder, and mustard. Cover, shake well, and chill.

Place spinach in a large salad bowl. Top with apple, raisins, peanuts and green onions. Pour dressing over salad and toss.

Serves 4-6.

Salad with Avocado Dressing

Salad
· 1 head lettuce, torn into bite-size pieces
· 3 tomatoes, cut into bite-size pieces
· 1 bunch green onions, chopped
· 1 can black olives, sliced
· 1 c. grated cheddar cheese
· Corn chips

Dressing
· ½ c. mashed avocado
· 1 Tbsp. lemon juice
· ½ c. sour cream
· ⅓ c. Miracle Whip®
· 1 clove garlic, crushed
· ½ tsp. sugar
· ½ tsp. chili powder
· ¼ tsp. salt
· ¼ tsp. Tabasco® sauce

Combine all ingredients for avocado dressing and mix well.

In large bowl, combine lettuce, tomatoes, green onions, olives, and cheddar cheese. Toss lightly with dressing. Top with slightly crushed corn chips. Serve immediately.

Note – Dressing does not keep well; should be used the same day as prepared.

Serves 6.

Sexy Italian Salad

· 2 Tbsp. Extra-virgin olive oil
· 2 Tbsp. Balsamic vinegar
· ½ c. Parmigiano-Reggiano cheese
· 1 head romaine lettuce
· Sea salt and freshly cracked pepper, to taste

Wash, dry, and tear lettuce and place in a large bowl. Pour olive oil over salad and toss lightly. Pour vinegar over salad and toss lightly. Grate cheese over lettuce (use products imported from Italy for best flavor). Sprinkle with salt and pepper. Mix salad. Serve immediately.

Sunshine Salad

Salad
· Grapefruit sections, chilled
· Avocado slices
· Grapes, seeded and halved
· Bananas, sliced
· Leaf lettuce

Orange Vinaigrette
· ½ can (6 oz.) of frozen orange juice concentrate, thawed
· ¼ c. honey
· 2 Tbsp. vinegar
· 1 tsp. salt
· ⅔ c. salad oil
· 1 Tbsp. poppy seeds

In blender or food processor, combine orange juice, honey, vinegar, and salt. Cover and blend. Blend at medium speed while slowly adding oil. Blend until thick. Stir in poppy seeds and chill until ready to serve.

Arrange fruit and avocado on bed of lettuce or in individual servings. Pour dressing over.

For larger groups, you may also toss with the dressing in a clear glass bowl and arrange lettuce leaves around edges.

Easy Greek Salad

· 10 c. torn mixed salad greens or romaine
· 3 medium tomatoes, cut into wedges
· 2 cucumbers, halved lengthwise and thinly sliced
· 1 small red onion, thinly sliced
· 1 small jar roasted red peppers, sliced into strips
· ½ c. pitted kalamata olives
· ½ c. (2 oz) crumbled Feta cheese

Greek Vinaigrette
· 2 Tbsp. olive oil or salad oil
· 2 Tbsp. lemon juice
· 2 tsp. snipped fresh oregano or ½ tsp. dried oregano, crushed
· ⅛ tsp. salt
· ⅛ tsp. black pepper

Combine all vinaigrette ingredients in a screw top jar. Cover and shake well.

In a salad bowl, combine salad greens, tomatoes, cucumbers, onion, red peppers, olives, and crumbled cheese. Add Greek vinaigrette; toss to coat.

Note—Serve with Pita bread wedges.

Serves 6-8.

Cornbread Salad

Topping
· 1 c. mayonnaise
· 1 package of ranch dressing mix
· 1 c. sour cream

Mix together and refrigerate.

Prepare 1 (7 ½-8 oz.) corn bread mix as directed. Let cool.

Crumble corn bread into 9x13-inch glass baking dish.

Salad
· 1 can pinto beans, rinsed and drained
· 1 green bell pepper, diced
· 1 medium tomato, seeded and diced
· ½ c. grated cheddar cheese
· 6 slices crisp bacon, crumbled
· 1 (15 oz.) can sweet corn, drained

Garnish
· 1 small can black olives, sliced
· 2 green onions, sliced thinly (whites and green tops)
· ½ c. grated cheddar cheese

Prepare salad ingredients, but don't assemble until ready to serve. On top of cornbread, layer salad ingredients in order as listed.

Spread topping over salad and garnish with sliced black olives, green onions, and grated cheddar cheese.

Greek Salad

· 1 lb. sliced mushrooms
· 1 can (2 ¼ oz.) sliced ripe olives
· 1 bunch green onions, chopped
· 8 oz. grated Swiss cheese
· ½ c. white vinegar
· ½ c. salad oil
· 1 Tbsp. Cavender's® Greek Seasoning
· ¼ tsp. sugar

Combine mushrooms, olives, green onions, and Swiss cheese in salad bowl.

In separate bowl, combine vinegar, oil, Cavender's® seasoning, and sugar; mix well.

Combine both mixtures and let stand in refrigerator covered for at least three hours before serving.

Serves 6-8.

The Best Spinach Salad

· 1 c. mayonnaise
· 1 c. salad oil
· ⅔ c. grated Parmesan cheese
· 1 tsp. salt
· 1 tsp. garlic powder
· 1 Tbsp. sugar
· ¼ c. wine vinegar
· 2 lbs. fresh spinach
· 1 purple onion, chopped
· 1 lb. bacon, cooked and crumbled
· 2 hard cooked eggs, chopped

Optional
· ¼ c. slivered almonds
· 2 Tbsp. sugar

Mix together mayonnaise, salad oil, cheese, salt, garlic powder, sugar, and wine vinegar. Toss with spinach and onion. Top with bacon and eggs.

Sauté almonds in sugar over medium heat. Spread on foil to cool. Sprinkle on salad.

This recipe serves 12-16.

Italian Salad

· Red onion
· Green bell pepper
· Cherry tomatoes (about 10)
· Feta cheese
· 8 pitted olives, chopped
· Stale bread or French stick
· Salt
· Black pepper
· Olive oil
· Fresh basil (about 10 leaves), roughly chopped

Peel and slice red onions, separate rings, then cut in half. Remove core and seeds from pepper, then slice. Slice cherry tomatoes in half. Mix onions, peppers, chopped olives, tomatoes, basil together in a bowl.

Tear bread coarsely and crumble the Feta cheese; add and toss with olive oil. Season to taste with salt and pepper before serving.

7 Layer Salad

· 1 head of lettuce, chopped
· 1 (16 oz.) bag of frozen sweet peas, thawed
   and dried with paper towel
· 1 bundle of green onions, thinly sliced
   (garnish top of the dish with stems)
· ½ head of cauliflower, cut into bite size pieces
· 1 c. mayonnaise (or more if you prefer)
· 1 c. sharp or mild cheese, shredded
· 8 strips of bacon, cooked and crumbled, divided

Fry bacon in a large, deep skillet. Cook over medium high heat until evenly brown. Crumble and set aside.

In a 4-quart dish, layer in order, lettuce, peas, green onions (not the stems), cauliflower, mayonnaise (spread with a spatula like icing), cheese, and bacon. On the side of the bowl, place the chopped green stems of the onions to form a circle. Inside this circle, make another thick circle of cheese and then inside that circle, place half of the crumbled bacon pieces.

Top individual helpings with other half of the bacon crumbles. Chill for 2 to 3 hours.

When ready to eat, dish out only the portion you will be serving; leave the remaining salad unstirred so it will stay fresher longer.

Chicken Salad

· 2 c. mayonnaise
· 8 c. cubed, cooked chicken
· 3 c. seedless green grapes, halved
· 3 c. seedless red grapes, halved
· ½ c. thinly sliced green onions
· 4 c. dried cranberries
· 2 Tbsp. garlic powder (optional)
· Salt and pepper to taste (optional)
· Cashew halves (optional)

In a large bowl, combine chicken, green grapes, red grapes, and green onions. Add salt, pepper, and garlic powder to taste. Stir in mayonnaise and mix well. Place the salad in the refrigerator and marinate for 2 hours, or overnight.

Mix in cranberries and cashew halves just before serving. Serve cold with croissants or rolls.

Chicken Carrot Luncheon Salad

· 3 c. cooked chicken, diced
· 1 c. carrots, shredded
· ¾ c. celery, diced
· ½ c. slivered almonds or chopped pecans
· 2 Tbsp. onion, finely chopped
· ¼ tsp. salt
· 1 c. mayonnaise
· 1 Tbsp. lemon juice
· 4 lettuce leaves
· Parsley, for garnish

Combine chicken, carrot, celery, nuts, onion, and salt. Mix lemon juice with mayonnaise and add to chicken mixture. Chill. Serve on lettuce cups.

Note—Serve with a fruit salad for a light summer dinner. Serve with soup and bread or crackers for a delicious lunch. Can also be served in a cantaloupe quarter.

Creamy Chicken Salad

· 2 lbs. boneless, skinless chicken breast halves
· ½ c. fat-free Miracle Whip®
· ½ c. plain, fat-free Greek yogurt
· 1 Tbsp. fresh lemon juice
· 1 Tbsp. white wine vinegar
· 1 Tbsp. Dijon mustard
· 1 tsp. honey
· ½ tsp. sea salt
· ½ tsp. ground black pepper
· ⅓ c. chopped celery
· ⅓ c. dried cranberries
· 10 - 12 coarsely chopped raw almonds
· 6 c. dark, leafy greens

Wrap chicken breast halves tightly in heavy-duty plastic wrap. Add the chicken to boiling water. Cover and simmer for 20 to 22 minutes. Remove from the pan, and let stand for 5 minutes. Unwrap chicken and shred; refrigerate for 30 minutes, or until cold.

Combine Miracle Whip® and the next seven ingredients (through black pepper) in a large bowl, stirring with a whisk until combined.

Add chicken, celery, cranberries, and almonds; toss well to coat. Cover and refrigerate at least 1 hour.

Serve over salad greens.

Serves 6.

Chicken and Rice Salad

· 3 c. cooked rice
· 2 whole chicken breasts, cooked and boned
· 1 (8 oz.) can small green peas, drained
· ½ c. onion, finely chopped
· 1 c. celery, finely chopped
· 1 tsp. salt
· 1 tsp. pepper
· ½ c. mayonnaise
· Dash Tabasco®

Cook rice as directed. Cook chicken breasts, skin, bone, and cut into pieces. Combine rice and chicken with peas, onion, celery, salt, pepper, mayonnaise, and Tabasco®.

Sauce
· 1 avocado, mashed
· ½ c. mayonnaise
· 1 c. sour cream
· ½ tsp. salt
· ½ tsp. onion salt
· ½ tsp. Worcestershire sauce
· ¼ tsp. garlic salt
· Dash of Tabasco®

In blender, mix all of the ingredients together and pour over chicken and rice mixture.

Refrigerate for at least 30 minutes.

Serves 6-8.

Artichoke Pasta Salad

· 6 oz. shell macaroni
· 2 jars (6 oz.) marinated artichoke hearts, undrained
· ¼ lb. mushrooms, cut in half
· 2 medium tomatoes, seeded and cut into bite-size pieces
· 1 c. small pitted ripe olives, cut in half
· Salt and pepper, to taste

Cook macaroni according to package directions. Drain, rinse with cold water, and drain again. Turn into large bowl.

Cut artichokes into bite-size pieces and add to macaroni (with artichoke liquid). Add mushrooms, tomatoes, and olives to pasta and toss gently.

Cover and refrigerate at least 4 hours or overnight. Before serving, season with salt and pepper.

Serves 8-10.

Deli-Style Pasta Salad

· 1 (7 oz.) package short cut pasta, such
    as farfalle, penne, or shells
· 6 oz. provolone cheese, cut into ¾-inch cubes
· 6 oz. sliced Genoa salami, cut into strips
· 1 small zucchini, thinly sliced
· 1 small onion, thinly sliced and separated into rings
· 1 ½ c. chopped green or red sweet pepper
· 1 (2 ¼ oz.) can sliced olives, drained
· 1 ¼ c. grated Parmesan cheese
· ¼ c. snipped fresh parsley

Dressing
· ½ c. olive oil
· ¼ c. white wine vinegar
· 1 ½ tsp. dry mustard
· 1 tsp. dried oregano, crushed
· 1 tsp. dried basil, crushed
· 1 clove garlic, minced
· 2 medium tomatoes cut into wedges
· Parsley sprigs (optional)

Cook macaroni according to package directions, then drain. Rinse with cold water, and then drain again.

In a large mixing bowl, combine macaroni, provolone cheese, salami, zucchini, onion, peppers, olives, Parmesan cheese, and snipped parsley.

Dressing: In a screw-top jar, combine olive oil, vinegar, dry mustard, oregano, basil, and garlic. Cover and shake well. Pour dressing over pasta mixture and toss lightly to coat. Cover and chill for 4 hours or overnight.

To serve, add tomato wedges and toss lightly. Transfer pasta mixture to a large salad bowl. If desired, garnish with parsley sprigs.

Cucumber-Avocado Soup

· 2 cucumbers, peeled and cut into chunks
· 1 avocado, peeled and cut into chunks
· 1 small bunch green onions
· 1 can chicken broth
· 1 c. light sour cream
· 1 c. plain yogurt
· 2 - 3 lemons, juiced
· 1 tsp. salt

Puree the first four ingredients in a food processor. Pour in a pitcher and add sour cream, plain yogurt, juice of lemons, and salt. Stir with a whisk, cover, and chill.

Serves 6 - 8 as a side.

Corn Chowder

· 4 slices bacon, cooked and diced
   (reserve bacon drippings)
· 1 carrot, grated
· 1 celery stalk, diced
· 1 medium red onion, diced
· 1 clove garlic, minced (or 1 tsp. jarred minced garlic)
· 2 Tbsp. fresh parsley, chopped (or 1 tsp. dried parsley)
· 1 tsp. pepper
· 4 Tbsp. flour
· 2 c. milk
· 1 can chicken stock (or 14 oz. chicken bouillon)
· 2 (14 oz.) cans corn, drained
· 1 (14 oz.) can creamed corn

Heat bacon drippings on medium heat and sauté corn, celery, onion, garlic, parsley, and pepper. Remove all to separate bowl, leaving about 2 Tbsp. bacon drippings in pan (add butter if there is none remaining).

Add flour to drippings and stir until absorbed. Gradually add stock or bouillon and milk, stirring to remove any lumps. Add vegetable mixture. When combined, add creamed corn and cooked bacon; cook over low heat for 30 minutes.

Cream of Zucchini Soup

· 3 medium-large zucchini, approximately 1 ½ lbs.
· ½ c. green onion, chopped, including tops
· 3 Tbsp. butter or margarine
· 4 c. chicken stock or canned chicken broth
· 1 ½ tsp. wine vinegar
· ¾ tsp. tarragon
· 4 Tbsp. farina (quick-cooking Cream of Wheat®)
· 1 c. sour cream
· Salt and pepper, to taste
· 3 dashes Tabasco® (optional)
· 1 Tbsp. parsley, minced

Wash zucchini and cut off ends, but do not peel. Cut into one-inch chunks.

In 3-qt. saucepan, cook onions in butter slowly until soft, but not brown. Add zucchini, stock or broth, vinegar, and tarragon, and heat to boiling. Stir in dry farina slowly. Simmer 25 minutes, then puree in blender.

Soup may be frozen or refrigerated at this point. Return to sauce pan and add sour cream. Heat slowly to simmer, stirring occasionally to blend cream. Do not boil. Season soup to taste with salt and pepper, adding Tabasco® if desired.

Serve in heated bowls with minced parsley sprinkled on top.

Fresh Mushroom Soup

· 1 lb. fresh mushrooms
· 3 Tbsp. butter
· 2 Tbsp. onion, minced
· 1 tsp. garlic powder
· 4 Tbsp. flour
· 6 chicken bouillon cubes
· 4 c. boiling water
· ¼ tsp. pepper
· 1 tsp. salt
· 1 ½ c. whipping cream

Wipe mushrooms with moist paper towels to clean. Chop stems and half of the caps. Slice remaining caps thinly. Melt butter in a large saucepan and sauté chopped portion of mushrooms with onion and garlic powder for 5 minutes. Blend in flour.

Dissolve bouillon cubes in boiling water and add to saucepan, stirring continuously until boiling. Add sliced mushrooms, pepper, and salt; cook over low heat for 15 minutes. Mix in cream and simmer until desired thickness.

Pink's Chicken a la Reine Soup

· ½ c. butter
· 1 c. flour
· 2 qts. half and half, or milk
· ½ lb. fresh mushrooms, sliced
· 1 medium yellow onion, diced
· 4 stalks celery, diced
· 2 lbs. chicken breasts, boiled and diced
· 1 c. white rice
· 1 tsp. Tabasco® sauce
· ¼ c. sherry
· 1 tsp. white pepper
· 1 tsp. salt
· Chicken bouillon, to taste

In a double boiler or crock-pot, combine butter, flour, half and half or milk. Simmer several hours, stirring occasionally.

Sauté mushrooms, onion, and celery, and add to soup.

Boil chicken breasts, dice and add to soup.

Cook rice according to package directions and add to soup. Add Tabasco® sauce, sherry, white pepper, salt, and bouillon. Cook until soup thickens.

Black-Eyed Pea Soup

· 1 lb. smoked sausage, sliced
· 2 tsp. vegetable oil
· 1 large onion, chopped
· 3 carrots, chopped
· 1 tsp. fresh garlic, chopped
· 2 celery ribs, chopped
· 1 large green bell pepper, chopped
· 4 c. frozen black-eyed peas
· 3 cans of beef or vegetable broth
· 1 (14 ½ oz.) can diced tomatoes, undrained
· ½ tsp. sea salt
· ½ tsp. freshly cracked pepper
· 1 (16 oz.) jar of salsa

Cook sausage in oil in a Dutch oven, stirring until brown. Remove sausage, reserve drippings.

Add onion and next four ingredients, sauté over medium-high heat until vegetables are tender.

Stir in sausage, peas, broth, tomatoes, and bring to a boil. Cover, reduce heat and simmer 45 minutes.

Add salt and pepper to taste. Stir in salsa.

Note – Great with cornmeal biscuits and sage butter, especially on New Year's Day!

Sopa de la Casa

· 8 slices bacon, diced
· 1 ¼ c. onion, finely chopped
· 1 ¼ c. celery, finely chopped
· 2 small green peppers, finely chopped
· 2 cloves garlic, minced
· 2 (14 ½ oz.) cans chicken broth
· 2 (16 oz.) cans refried beans
· ½ tsp. pepper
· 2 Tbsp. chili powder
· Shredded Monterey Jack cheese
· Tortilla chips

In soup pot, cook bacon until crisp. Drain half of bacon drippings. Add onion, celery, and green pepper. Cook until tender, then add garlic. Blend in chicken broth, refried beans, pepper, and chili powder. Bring to boil and remove from heat immediately.

Garnish with cheese and serve with chips or tostados.

Serves 8.

The Best Tortilla Soup

· 2 c. cooked chicken, skinned, boned, and chopped
· ¼ c. olive oil
· 1 - 2 fresh jalapeños, seeded, veined, and finely chopped
· 4 cloves garlic, peeled and minced
· 1 medium white or yellow onion, diced
· 2 cans diced tomatoes
· 1 can Rotel®
· 2 cans beef broth
· 2 cans chicken broth (reserved from boiling chicken)
· 1 - 2 cans chopped green chiles
· 2 cans tomato soup
· 1 can tomato juice
· 1 c. water
· 1 ½ tsp. ground cumin
· 10 corn tortillas or bag of tortilla chips, slightly crushed
· 2 Tbsp. oil to fry tortillas
· 2 Tbsp. fresh cilantro, chopped (as garnish (optional))
· Avocado, peeled and diced (as garnish (optional))
· Sour cream (as garnish (optional))

Cook chicken breasts in boiling water until done. Remove chicken from broth, allow chicken to cool a bit, then skin and bone. Cut chicken into bite size pieces and set aside. Skim fat off top of remaining chicken broth and set aside.

In the bottom of a big stockpot, heat olive oil over medium heat. Add jalapeños, garlic, and onion and sauté until tender. Add the next nine ingredients and bring soup to a simmer.

Fry corn tortillas in a skillet with a small amount of oil, cool slightly, then cut into strips.

When ready to serve, add cooked chicken back to soup and stir lightly. Place tortilla strips or chips in individual bowls, top with soup, and garnish with fresh cilantro, diced avocado, and sour cream.

Serves 6 - 8.

O Asian Fusion's Spicy Shrimp Noodle Soup

· 4 c. chicken stock
· ½ Tbsp. pork fat (bacon drippings)
· 4 oz. rice noodles
· 1 lb. of shrimp (16 - 20 count)
· Sriracha hot sauce, to taste
· 2 Tbsp. chives, chopped
· 1 Tbsp. cilantro, chopped
· 4 Tbsp. bean sprouts

Bring chicken stock to a boil. Add pork fat and rice noodles and cook until tender. Add shrimp and cook until pink. Add Sriracha hot sauce with freshly chopped chives and bean sprouts.

Serves 4-6.

Gigi's Vegetable Soup

· 2 cans chicken broth
· 1 red potato, diced
· 1 turnip, diced
· 1 yellow squash, grated
· 1 zucchini, grated
· 2 large carrots, grated
· 1 onion, diced
· 1 stalk of celery, diced
· 1 (12 oz.) can of corn
· ½ c. cabbage, shredded
· 1 can of English green peas
· 1 can of diced tomatoes
· 8 oz. of small pasta
· 1 can tomato puree or sauce
· 1 c. V8® juice, low-sodium
· Salt and pepper, to taste

Pour chicken broth into Dutch oven. Add all ingredients and bring to a boil. Reduce heat to low and simmer 45 minutes.

Vegetarian Entrées

Wine Pairings with Vegetarian Entrées

Pinot Gris

Sauvignon Blanc

Zinfandel

Chianti

Pair red wines with heartier fare like bean dishes, enchiladas, etc., while reserving the lighter whites for dishes based on green vegetables.

Lean, clean white wines with crisp acidity seem to pair best with delicate entrées fashioned from fresh green vegetables.

So, if the centerpiece of your meatless meal is green and fresh, whether it's a spinach quiche, a vegetarian risotto or a bowl of green beans, break out the white wines and bubblies and serve them well chilled. (Just remember to avoid vinegar-based salad dressings, which "fight" with any wine.)

Fettuccine Alfredo

· Half-pint whipping cream
· 8 oz. sour cream
· 8 oz. Parmesan cheese
· 2 tsp. garlic salt
· ½ tsp. coarsely ground black pepper
· ¼ c. butter
· 12 oz. fettuccine noodles
· 1 tsp. snipped parsley (optional)

Mix whipping cream, sour cream, and Parmesan cheese together. Add garlic salt, pepper and parsley.

Boil noodles according to package directions. Drain. Add butter to noodles. Pour cream sauce over noodles and serve.

Serves 6.

Last Minute Lasagna

· 1 (26 oz.) jar pasta sauce
· 1 (30 oz.) bag frozen cheese ravioli, thawed
· 1 (10 oz.) box frozen spinach, thawed and squeezed dry
· 1 (8 oz.) bag shredded mozzarella cheese
· ½ c. grated cheddar cheese

Preheat oven to 350°.

Coat a 9×13-inch baking dish with cooking spray. Spoon ⅓ of the sauce in dish; arrange 12 ravioli on top. Sprinkle spinach over ravioli. Top with half of each cheese. Cover with another layer of ravioli and then top with remaining sauce and cheeses.

Cover and bake for 25 minutes. Uncover and bake 5 to 10 minutes more or until bubbly.

Pasta with Eggplant Sauce

· 1 firm eggplant
· 1 onion, diced
· 3 garlic cloves, minced
· 1 red bell pepper, diced
· Red pepper flakes (optional)
· ¼ c. olive oil
· 2 Tbsp. capers
· 1 or 2 (6 oz.) jars marinated artichoke hearts, drained
· 1 (8 oz.) can chopped tomatoes or fresh tomatoes
· 1 (8 oz.) can tomato sauce
· ½ c. fresh basil, chopped
· 3 Tbsp. fresh oregano, chopped
· 1 lb. rigatoni or other substantial pasta
· Freshly grated Parmesan cheese, to taste

Slice eggplant into circles and sprinkle with salt. Allow to set for about 30 minutes to draw out any bitterness. Brush circles with olive oil and grill or broil. When cool enough to touch, cube the eggplant.

In large saucepan, sauté onions, garlic, and red bell pepper in oil until translucent. Add eggplant, capers, and artichokes. Cook for a few minutes. Add tomatoes, salt, and pepper to taste, tomato sauce, basil and oregano. Simmer, partly covered, until thick.

Serve over rigatoni or other pasta with freshly grated parmesan.

Lemon Zest Whole Wheat Penne

· 14 oz. whole wheat penne pasta
· 2 Tbsp. Parmesan cheese
· Zest of 1 lemon
· Olive oil
· Salt and pepper, to taste

Cook pasta according to package directions in salted water. Drain, reserving some of the cooking liquid (about 1 cup).

Return the pasta to pan and drizzle with olive oil. While stirring, add the Parmesan cheese and the zest of one lemon. Add salt and pepper, to taste.

White Spaghetti

· 1 c. olive oil
· ⅓ c. green olives, chopped
· ¼ c. pepperoncini peppers, chopped
· 1 tsp. Italian seasoning
· 8 oz. angel hair pasta

Sauté olives and pepperoncini in olive oil on low heat for 20 minutes. Add Italian seasoning and remove from heat.

Serve over al dente angel hair pasta.

Note – Great with crusty bread and an Italian salad.

Bart and Nadia's Eggplant Parmigiana

· 1 egg, slightly beaten
· 1 c. milk
· 1 Tbsp. vegetable oil
· 1 c. flour
· 2 medium eggplants, peeled and cut into ½-inch slices
· Hot vegetable oil
· 1 (28 oz.) can tomato sauce
· 1 (12 oz.) can tomato paste
· 1 (16 oz.) can tomatoes, drained
· ¼ c. Burgundy wine
· 1 tsp. dried whole oregano
· ½ tsp. dried whole basil
· ¼ tsp. dried whole thyme
· ¼ tsp. garlic salt
· 10 - 16 oz. sliced Mozzarella cheese
· Grated Parmesan cheese, to taste

Preheat oven to 350°.

Combine milk, egg, 1 Tbsp. vegetable oil; gradually add to flour, beating until smooth.

Dip eggplant in flour mixture; fry in hot oil until golden, adding oil as necessary. Drain well on paper towels; set aside.

Combine next eight ingredients in medium saucepan, mixing well. Simmer sauce 10 minutes.

Arrange half of eggplant slices in a lightly greased 13×9×2-inch baking dish. Top with half of Mozzarella slices. Spoon half of tomato mixture over cheese. Repeat layers. Top with Parmesan cheese.

Bake at 350° for 30 to 40 minutes, or until sauce is bubbly.

Serves 6 - 8.

Soba Noodle Salad with Tofu and Green Beans

· 8 oz. green beans, trimmed and cut into 2-inch pieces
· 6 oz. soba noodles
· 6 oz. tofu, cut into ½-inch cubes
· 3 Tbsp. fresh lime juice
· 2 Tbsp. soy sauce
· 2 tsp. toasted sesame oil
· 2 scallions, minced

In a large pot of boiling, salted water, cook 8 oz. green beans, cut into 2-inch pieces, approximately 4 minutes. Use a slotted spoon to transfer to a colander. In the same pot, cook 6 oz. soba noodles according to package instructions; drain well (do not rinse).

Whisk together fresh lime juice, soy sauce, and toasted sesame oil. Pour half the dressing over tofu; toss gently to coat.

In a large bowl, toss remaining dressing with noodles, green beans, and 2 minced scallions. Sprinkle tofu on top. Let cool.

Zucchini-Ricotta Main Dish

· 3 c. zucchini (about ¾ lb.), cut in ¼-inch slices
· 4 Tbsp. butter, divided
· 1 Tbsp. olive oil
· 1 ½ c. onion, finely chopped
· 1 garlic clove, minced
· ¼ tsp. basil
· Pinch nutmeg, salt, and pepper
· 1 (28 oz.) can whole peeled tomatoes, drained and quartered
· 1 c. Mozzarella cheese, grated

Filling
· 1 egg
· 1 c. ricotta cheese
· 1 Tbsp. parsley
· Salt
· Pepper
· 1 c. Mozzarella cheese, grated

Preheat oven to 375°.

Filling: Add beaten egg to ricotta cheese and mix well. Add chopped parsley, pepper, and salt to taste. Stir in Mozzarella cheese.

Zucchini: In large skillet over medium heat, sauté zucchini in 2 Tbsp. butter and olive oil 5 to 7 minutes until tender-crisp. Drain on paper towels and set aside.

Add 2 Tbsp. butter to skillet and cook onion for 8 minutes; stir in garlic, basil, nutmeg, tomatoes, and salt and pepper to taste. Cook over medium heat until most of the moisture evaporates.

In shallow baking pan, arrange half of reserved zucchini. Pour over half tomato mixture. Spread on filling. Repeat layers of zucchini and tomatoes. Sprinkle on Mozzarella.

Bake at 375° for 40 minutes. Let stand 5 minutes before serving.

Serves 6.

Note – The key is cooking zucchini ONLY to tender-crisp stage!

Spaghetti Squash Casserole

· 1 medium spaghetti squash
· 1 c. chopped onion
· 1 c. shredded cheese
· 1 c. shredded zucchini
· 1 c. shredded carrots
· ½ c. chopped green bell pepper
· 1 c. tomato sauce or prepared spaghetti sauce
· 1 - 2 cloves garlic, minced
· ½ tsp. salt
· ½ tsp. pepper
· ½ tsp. basil
· ½ c. Parmesan cheese

Preheat oven to 375°.

Prepare spaghetti squash by one of the following methods:

Microwave: Pierce spaghetti squash with a fork in several places. Place on paper towel and cook 15 minutes, turning 4 times; let stand 3 minutes. If shell doesn't give to pressure, cook 2 to 3 minutes more. After baking, split squash lengthwise, scoop out seeds and run fork over inside of squash to release spaghetti-like strands.

Conventional oven: Pierce spaghetti squash with a fork in several places. Cut lengthwise and remove seeds. Place cut side down on a cookie sheet. Bake at 350° for 45 minutes. Turn squash and bake until skin is tender. Run fork over inside of squash to release spaghetti-like strands.

While spaghetti squash is cooking, prepare other vegetables and cheese with food processor. Combine spaghetti squash, onions, cheese, zucchini, carrots, bell pepper, sauce, garlic, and spices in a casserole. Top with Parmesan cheese. Bake 40 minutes, uncovered at 375°.

Serves 6 - 8.

Ratatouille

· ¼ c. vegetable oil or olive oil
· 2 onions, thinly sliced
· 2 green bell peppers, thinly sliced
· 1 red bell pepper, thinly sliced
· 2 eggplants, peeled and cubed
· 3 large zucchini, cut into fingers
· 4 cloves garlic, minced
· ½ lb. fresh mushrooms, sliced
· 4 cans Italian tomatoes, drained (reserve a
    little juice to add with tomatoes)
· ¼ c. fresh parsley, minced
· ½ tsp. basil
· Garlic salt, salt and pepper, to taste

In heavy skillet, sauté onions and peppers in oil until transparent. Remove vegetables to large pot.

In the oil, stir-fry quickly each vegetable separately - eggplant, zucchini, fresh garlic, and mushrooms. As prepared, remove each vegetable to large pot with onions and peppers. Add tomatoes, parsley, basil, garlic salt, salt and pepper. Cook slowly for 20 minutes. Be careful not to overcook!

Serve hot or cold.

Chicken Entrées

Wine Pairings with Chicken Entrées

Bordeaux (Cabernet Sauvignon, Merlot), Burgundy (Pinot Noir), Beaujolais and Dolcetto, fruity Zinfandel…all match well with this versatile bird; but so do Chardonnay, Pinot Blanc, and Riesling.

One of the most obvious exceptions to the traditional rule about "red wine with red meat, white wine with white meat" is roast chicken, indisputably a "white meat" but one that works just as well and perhaps even better with red wine than white.

With other chicken dishes, consider the sauce and the preparation as keys to the match: Light chicken-breast sautés or cream sauces may tilt the equation toward a white. Tomatoey, cheesy entrees like chicken cacciatore and its kin call for a dry red, perhaps an Italian (Chianti, Bardolino, Valpolicella) to make an ethnic match.

Chicken Divan

· 2 packages frozen chopped broccoli (or
    spears) cooked according to directions
· 2 c. cooked chicken breast, cut into equal-size pieces
· 2 cans cream of chicken soup
· 1 c. mayonnaise
· 1 Tbsp. lemon juice
· ¼ to ½ tsp. curry powder
· ½ c. cheddar cheese, grated
· ½ c. soft bread crumbs
· 1 tsp. butter, melted

Preheat oven to 350°.

In a lightly greased 2-quart baking dish, place a layer of broccoli. Combine soup, mayonnaise, lemon juice, curry, and spread on top of broccoli. Place a layer of chicken on top of soup mixture. Sprinkle with cheese. Mix bread crumbs and butter then spread on top of cheese.

Bake uncovered at 350° for 30 minutes.

Variations for bread crumb topping: Melt ½ cup butter. Mix in ½ of 8 oz. package of Herb Dressing. Spread on top of cheese.

Serves 6-8.

Chicken with Artichoke Hearts

· 3 lbs. chicken breasts, boned and skinned
· 1 tsp. salt
· ½ tsp. paprika
· ¼ tsp. pepper
· ¼ c. plus 2 Tbsp. butter, divided
· 1 (9 oz.) package frozen artichoke hearts, thawed
· ¼ lb. fresh mushrooms, sliced
· 2 Tbsp. flour
· ⅔ c. chicken broth
· 3 Tbsp. dry sherry or Rosé wine

Preheat oven at 375°.

Sprinkle chicken with paprika, salt, and pepper. Melt ¼ cup butter in a large skillet. Brown chicken uncovered on low heat then transfer to greased 2-quart casserole dish, reserving chicken drippings in skillet. Arrange artichoke hearts between chicken breasts; set aside.

Add remaining butter to reserved drippings then melt over low heat. Add mushrooms and sauté. Stir flour into mushrooms, gradually adding broth and sherry. Cook over medium heat, stirring constantly until thickened and bubbly, about 5 minutes.

Pour sauce over chicken. Cover and bake for 40 minutes.

Serves 6-8.

Chicken and Rice Casserole

· 4 whole chicken breasts (or 1 whole chicken)
· 1 c. dry sherry
· 1 c. water
· ½ c. celery, chopped
· 1 small onion, chopped
· 1 ½ tsp. salt
· ½ tsp. curry
· 1 (6 oz.) box wild and long grain rice
· 1 lb. fresh mushrooms or 1 (8 oz.) can mushrooms
· ½ c. butter
· 1 c. sour cream
· 1 (10 ¾ oz.) can cream of mushroom soup
· Slivered almonds

Preheat oven to 350°.

Bring chicken and next six ingredients to a boil. Cover and simmer for 1 hour. Skin, bone, and cut chicken into bite-size pieces. Strain liquid and use to cook rice.

Sauté mushrooms in butter and mix with soup and sour cream. Add rice and chicken. Put in a 3-quart casserole or two 1 ½-quart casseroles and sprinkle with slivered almonds.

Bake at 350° for 1 hour.

Serves 8-10.

Chicken and Artichoke Casserole

· 2 large chicken breasts, boned
· 1 bay leaf
· 1 c. sherry or white wine
· 2 c. artichoke hearts
· ½ lb. fresh mushrooms, chopped
· ½ c. green onions, chopped
· 2 Tbsp. butter
· Garlic salt
· 2 (8 ½ oz.) cans artichoke hearts, drained
    and quartered (not marinated)
· ¾ c. mayonnaise
· ½ c. sour cream
· 1 c. Parmesan cheese
· Salt and pepper, to taste

Cook chicken until tender with bay leaf, ½ cup sherry, salt and pepper. Cut chicken into bite-size pieces then place chicken and artichoke hearts in 2-quart casserole.

Sauté mushrooms and green onions in butter. Mix remaining ingredients except ½ cup of Parmesan cheese and combine with sautéed onions and mushrooms. Spread mixture over top of chicken and artichoke hearts. Top with remaining ½ cup of Parmesan cheese.

Bake at 350°, uncovered, for 20 minutes.

Serves 4-6.

Easy Chicken Pot Pie

· 2 (10 ¾ oz.) cans cream of chicken or
    mushroom soup, undiluted
· 1 c. milk
· ¼ tsp. dried thyme
· ¼ tsp. pepper
· 2 c. cooked chicken (from the deli)
· 1 (16 oz.) package frozen mixed vegetables of your choice
· Sliced jarred or fresh mushrooms,
    sautéed in 1 Tbsp. butter
· 1 (12 oz.) can refrigerated biscuits

Preheat oven at 350°.

Combine all ingredients, except biscuits, and put in a
greased 9×12-inch casserole pan. Bake about 15 to 20
minutes at 350°.

Remove from oven and put biscuits on top. Increase oven
to 425°. Return dish to the oven and bake until the biscuits
are golden.

Serves 4-6.

Chicken with Wild Rice

· 2 (6.5 oz.) boxes of Long-Grain and Wild Rice
· 2 c. of chicken broth
· 2 c. of white wine
· 2 (8 oz.) cans of tomato sauce
· 2 large onions, diced
· 12 chicken breasts
· 1 Tbsp. olive oil
· Salt and pepper, to taste

Preheat oven to 375°.

Brown the onions in olive oil. Mix with uncooked rice
and place in a greased casserole dish. Cover with broth,
wine, and tomato sauce. Cover casserole and bake for 45
minutes.

Season chicken with salt and pepper and tuck chicken into
the baked rice mixture, reduce the oven temperature to
350º and bake for additional 30 minutes.

Serves 10-12.

Billy Tubbs' Sherry Chicken

· 4 large chicken breasts, with skin
· 1 can of condensed cream of mushroom soup
· 3 oz. can of mushrooms with liquid
· 1 c. sour cream
· ½ c. cooking sherry
· Paprika

Preheat oven to 350°.

Place chicken, skin-side up, in 11×7-inch baking dish.

Combine soup, mushrooms with liquid, sour cream, and sherry. Pour over chicken. Sprinkle generously with paprika.

Bake at 350° for 1 hour to 1 hour and 15 minutes.

Serves 4.

Chicken Breasts in Sour Cream Sauce

· 8 chicken breasts
· 1 Tbsp. cinnamon and sugar mixture
· 1 tsp. granulated garlic
· ¼ tsp. nutmeg
· 1 Tbsp. soy sauce
· 1 Tbsp. honey
· ¼ c. Sauterne
· 2 shallots, sliced
· ¼ lb. fresh mushrooms, sliced
· ½ stick butter
· 4 Tbsp. flour
· 2 c. half and half
· 2 c. sour cream
· Salt and pepper, to taste

Preheat oven to 350°.

Season chicken with cinnamon and sugar mixture, nutmeg, and garlic. Cover with soy sauce, honey, and wine. Season with salt and pepper. Place in casserole dish, cover, and bake for 1 hour.

Sauté shallots and mushrooms in the butter until tender. Add flour and cream and stir until the mixture thickens. Add sour cream. Warm, but do not boil. Pour sauce over chicken and serve.

Serves 6-8.

Dijon Chicken

· 8 chicken breasts, boned and skinned
· 1 ½ sticks butter
· 8 Tbsp. Dijon mustard
· 1 ½ c. ground pecans
· 2 Tbsp. olive oil
· 1 ½ c. sour cream

Preheat oven to 350°.

In a skillet, melt 1 stick of butter. Remove from heat and whisk in 6 Tbsp. Dijon mustard. Dip each breast in butter mixture then in ground pecans.

In large, heavy skillet melt the remaining butter and oil. Sauté the chicken on both sides until golden brown. Remove chicken to a shallow baking dish; cover with foil; bake for 30 minutes or until tender.

Pour off butter and pecans from skillet and deglaze with sour cream, scraping up brown bits from the bottom of skillet. Whisk remaining mustard into sauce and season with salt and pepper, to taste. Transfer chicken to platter and pour sauce over chicken.

Serves 8.

One-Dish Greek Lemon Chicken and Potatoes

· 1 broiler chicken or 4 chicken breasts
· 1 ½ Tbsp. oregano
· 1 ½ c. water
· 1 tsp. fresh garlic
· Juice of 3 lemons
· Olive oil to coat
· 6 large potatoes
· Salt and pepper, to taste

Preheat oven to 350°.

Cut potatoes into quarters. Place chicken and potatoes in glass dish. Salt and pepper the chicken and potatoes, then add garlic and oregano. Squeeze lemon juice over entire dish. Add olive oil to coat. Pour water on bottom of dish.

Bake 45 minutes or until golden, uncover for the last 15 minutes.

Note – Serve with a Greek salad and crusty bread.

Serves 4 - 6.

Rolled Chicken Washington

· ½ c. fresh mushrooms (or 3 oz. jar
    mushrooms, drained), chopped
· 2 Tbsp. butter or margarine
· 2 Tbsp. flour
· ½ c. light cream
· ½ tsp. salt
· Dash cayenne pepper
· 1 ¼ c. shredded sharp cheddar cheese
· 6 or 7 whole boneless chicken breasts
· Flour
· 2 eggs, lightly beaten
· ¾ c. fine bread crumbs

Preheat oven to 325°.

To prepare cheese filling, cook mushrooms in butter about 5 minutes; blend in flour, add cream, salt, and cayenne. Cook and stir until mixture becomes thick. Stir in cheese; continue stirring over low heat until cheese is melted. Pour mixture into pie plate. Cover and chill about 1 hour. Cut cheese into 6 or 7 equal portions; shape it into short sticks.

Remove skin from chicken breasts. Place the chicken breasts (boned side up) between 2 pieces of plastic wrap, overlapping meat where chicken breast is split. Pound chicken with wooden mallet to form a ¼-inch thick cutlet. Peel off plastic wrap. Sprinkle meat with salt and pepper.

Place a cheese stick on each chicken breast. Tuck in the sides; roll chicken as for jellyroll. Press to seal well. (Use toothpicks, if necessary). Cover chicken rolls with flour, dip in eggs, and then roll in breadcrumbs. Chill 1 hour (or prepare a day ahead and chill overnight).

About 1 hour before serving time, fry rolls in deep, hot fat (375°) for 5 minutes or until crisp and golden; drain on paper towels. Place rolls in shallow baking dish and bake in slow oven (325°) about 30 to 45 minutes. Serve on a warm platter.

Serves 6 - 7.

Brent Venables' Bruschetta Chicken

· ½ c. all-purpose flour
· 2 eggs, lightly beaten
· 4 chicken breast halves, boneless and skinless (1 lb.)
· ¼ c. grated Parmesan cheese
· ¼ c. dry bread crumbs
· 1 Tbsp. butter or margarine, melted
· 2 large tomatoes, seeded and chopped
· 3 Tbsp. minced fresh basil
· 2 garlic cloves, minced
· 1 Tbsp. olive or vegetable oil
· ½ tsp. salt
· ¼ tsp. pepper

Preheat oven to 375°.

Place flour and eggs in separate shallow bowls. Dip chicken in flour, then in eggs; place in a greased 9×13-inch baking dish.

Combine the Parmesan cheese, bread crumbs, and butter; sprinkle over chicken.

Loosely cover baking dish with foil. Bake at 375° for 20 minutes. Uncover; bake 5 to 10 minutes longer or until top is browned.

Meanwhile, in a bowl, combine the remaining ingredients and spoon over the chicken. Return to the oven for 3 to 5 minutes or until tomato mixture is heated through.

Serves 4.

Chicken Kiev

· ⅔ c. butter
· 1 c. fine dry bread crumbs
· 2 Tbsp. Parmesan cheese
· 1 tsp. basil leaves
· 1 Tbsp. oregano leaves
· ½ tsp. garlic salt
· ¼ tsp. salt
· 1 ½ lbs. boneless chicken breasts
· ¼ c. dry white wine
· ¼ c. green onion, chopped
· ¼ c. parsley, chopped

Preheat oven to 375°.

On wax paper combine bread crumbs, cheese, basil, oregano, garlic salt, and salt. Dip chicken in butter. Roll in crumbs to coat. Bake in square baking dish 50 to 60 minutes until golden brown and tender.

Add wine, green onion, and parsley to remaining butter and pour over chicken for 5 more minutes in oven.

Serves 4.

Chicken Rollups

· 4 chicken breasts, medium
· 12 oz. block of Swiss cheese
· 1 c. flour
· 2 tsp. salt
· 2 tsp. black pepper
· ½ c. white wine
· 16 oz. chicken broth
· 6 oz. fresh mushrooms, sliced

Preheat oven to 350°.

Place flour, salt, and black pepper in a gallon-size plastic zip bag.

Slice chicken breast along one side to create a pouch. Place 3 oz. of cheese in each breast and close opening with toothpicks.

Shake chicken in flour mixture until coated. Lightly sauté chicken. Once browned, place chicken in casserole dish.

Sprinkle flour into skillet until oil is absorbed. Slowly stir in chicken broth until flour is well blended. Add sliced mushrooms and wine. Allow mixture to simmer for 5 minutes. Pour mixture over chicken and cover. Bake at 350° for 1 hour.

Serves 4.

Company Chicken from Peggy Elder

· 4 - 6 split chicken breast halves, with bone and skin
· Soft garlic and herb cheese, one wedge per breast
· 1 Tbsp. light olive oil
· Salt and pepper, to taste

Preheat oven to 375°.

Rinse chicken breasts and open a pocket from the top by running your finger between the skin and meat. Be careful not to go all the way through to the end. Insert one wedge of cheese (or 1-2 oz. broken into 3 or 4 pieces) and distribute evenly between skin and meat. Place meat on baking pan lined with foil. Sprinkle with a little olive oil, salt, and pepper.

Bake at 375° for 40 to 45 minutes. Remove from oven and loosely cover with foil. Let rest 10 minutes.

Place slices on a bed of mixed rice and add any juices that are in the pan.

Serves 4-6.

Chicken Kabobs Supreme

· 2 whole chicken breasts, skinned and boned
· ½ c. vegetable oil
· ¼ c. soy sauce
· ¼ c. light corn syrup
· 1 Tbsp. sesame seeds
· 2 Tbsp. lemon juice
· ¼ tsp. garlic powder
· ¼ tsp. ground ginger
· 1 small pineapple, cut into 1-inch pieces
· 1 large green bell pepper, cut into 1-inch pieces
· 2 medium onions, quartered
· 3 zucchinis, cut into 1-inch pieces
· ½ lb. fresh mushroom caps

Cut the chicken breasts into 1-inch pieces; set aside.

Combine next seven ingredients; mix well. Add chicken. Cover and marinate at least 2 hours in refrigerator.

Alternate chicken and other ingredients on skewers. Grill until done.

Serves 4.

Chicken Penne Pasta

· 1 ½ c. uncooked penne pasta
· 1 lb. boneless skinless chicken thighs, cut into 1-inch
   pieces
· ½ c. each – chopped onion, green bell pepper, and sweet
   red bell pepper
· 1 tsp. each – dried basil, oregano, and parsley flakes
· ½ tsp. salt
· ½ tsp. crushed red pepper flakes
· 1 Tbsp. canola oil
· 1 ½ tsp. minced garlic
· 1 can (14.5 oz.) diced tomatoes, undrained
· 3 Tbsp. tomato paste
· ¾ c. chicken broth
· 2 c. (8 oz.) shredded part-skim Mozzarella cheese
· ½ c. grated Romano cheese

Preheat oven to 350°.

Cook pasta according to package directions.

In a large saucepan, sauté the chicken, onion, peppers, and seasonings in oil until chicken is no longer pink. Add garlic and cook 1 minute longer.

In a blender, combine tomatoes and tomato paste; cover and process until blended. Add to the chicken mixture. Stir in broth. Bring to a boil. Reduce heat; cover and simmer for 10 to 15 minutes or until sauce is slightly thickened. Drain pasta and toss with chicken mixture.

Spoon half of the mixture into a greased 2-qt. baking dish. Sprinkle with half of the Mozzarella and Romano cheeses. Repeat layers.

Cover and bake at 350° for 30 minutes. Uncover; bake 15 to 20 minutes longer or until heated through.

Serves 4.

Sweet and Sour Chicken

· 1 (8 oz.) bottle Russian dressing
· 1 envelope dry onion soup mix (4-servings size)
· 1 (l0 oz.) jar apricot preserves
· 1 chicken, cut up (or favorite pieces)

Crock-pot Method

Mix together dressing, soup mix, and preserves. Place chicken pieces in crockpot. Pour mixture over chicken. Cook in crock-pot on low for 8 hours.

Conventional Oven Method

Mix together dressing, soup mix, and preserves. Place chicken in baking dish and pour mixture over chicken. Cover with foil. Bake at 375° for 1 hour. Uncover and return to oven for 15 minutes.

Serves 4.

Chicken with Snow Peas

· 2 boneless and skinless chicken breasts
· 2 Tbsp. olive oil
· Salt and pepper, to taste
· 2 c. celery, sliced
· 1 c. onion, sliced
· 1 package frozen snow peas (or ½ lb. fresh)
· 1 c. chicken broth
· 2 Tbsp. cornstarch
· 2 tsp. sugar
· ½ tsp salt
· 2 Tbsp. soy sauce

Cut chicken into thin strips. Sauté chicken in oil for 2 to 3 minutes. Add salt, pepper, celery, onions, snow peas, and ¼ cup of the chicken broth. Cover and steam for 2 minutes. Remove cover and stir.

Blend remaining broth, cornstarch, sugar, salt and soy sauce. Stir broth mixture into chicken and vegetable mixture until thickened.

Serves 4.

Stir Fried Cashew Chicken

· 3 whole chicken breasts
· 3 Tbsp. soy sauce
· 2 Tbsp. sherry
· 2 tsp. cornstarch
· ¼ tsp. crushed red pepper
· ½ tsp. fresh ground ginger (optional)
· 1 garlic clove, minced
· Olive or salad oil
· ½ c. cashew nuts
· 1 red or green bell pepper, cut into strips
· 3 green onions, cut in 2-inch pieces
· ½ lb. fresh mushrooms, sliced
· ¼ lb. snow peas (optional)

Cut chicken breast into small pieces. In a bowl, stir together chicken and next six ingredients. Marinate for 15 to 20 minutes.

In a 12-inch skillet or wok, over medium heat, cook cashews in 1 Tbsp. hot oil, stirring until golden. Remove to small dish.

In the same skillet, add 2 Tbsp. oil and cook chicken mixture over medium-high heat, until nearly tender. Add vegetables and continue cooking until chicken is done and vegetables are tender-crisp. Sprinkle with cashews.

Serves 6.

Spanish Paella

· 2 pinches saffron
· 2 c. short grain rice
· 6 Tbsp. olive oil
· 6 chicken breasts, cut into chunks
· 5 oz. chorizo sausage, cut into chunks
· 16 uncooked shrimp, peeled and deveined
· 2 onions, chopped
· 4 cloves of garlic, chopped
· 1 Tbsp. Spanish paprika
· 1 c. green beans, chopped
· 1 c. frozen peas
· 5 c. chicken or vegetable stock
· 2 sweet red bell peppers, chopped
· 3 Tbsp. fresh parsley
· Paella pan (or flameproof casserole)
· 4 Tbsp. hot water

Put saffron threads in small bowl and pour in 4 Tbsp. of hot water; steep.

Heat 3 Tbsp. of oil in a 12-inch paella pan over medium-high heat. Add chicken, cook for 5 minutes until golden. Transfer to bowl. Add chorizo to pan and cook for 1 minute, or until crisp, then add to the chicken.

Heat 3 Tbsp. oil in the pan; add onions and cook for 2 minutes, then add garlic and paprika for 3 minutes until onions are soft. Add rice, beans, and peas to pan and stir until coated with oil.

Return chicken and chorizo to pan and stir in stock, saffron liquid (strained), salt and pepper, and bring to a boil, stirring. Reduce heat and simmer for 15 minutes, until rice is fluffy and absorbed the liquid. Add shrimp and peppers and continue stirring, adding more broth if needed.

Serve with fresh parsley sprinkled on top.

Serves 4-6.

Chicken Burritos

· 2 Tbsp. olive oil
· 1 medium onion, chopped
· 1 medium tomato, chopped
· 1 small green chile pepper, seeded and chopped
· 1 garlic clove, minced
· 2 ½ c. cooked chicken, cubed
· 1 (15 oz.) can refried beans
· 1 (8 oz.) jar picante sauce
· 12 flour tortillas
· Cheddar cheese, grated
· 1 head Romaine lettuce, shredded

In a medium skillet, heat oil, and sauté onion, tomato, green chile, and garlic until tender, about 10 minutes. Add chicken and heat through; keep warm.

In separate saucepans, heat beans, and picante sauce; keep warm.

On each tortilla, spread 1 Tbsp. beans, top with chicken, a little cheese, then roll up. Place on a plate lined with shredded lettuce and spoon 3 Tbsp. picante sauce over each.

Serves 6.

Chicken Enchiladas

· 3 large chicken breasts, cooked
· 1 c. onion, chopped
· 1 clove garlic, minced
· 2 Tbsp. butter
· 1 (16 oz.) can tomatoes, diced
· 1 (8 oz.) can tomato sauce
· ¼ c. chopped green chiles
· 1 tsp. sugar
· 1 tsp. ground cumin
· ½ tsp. salt
· ½ tsp. dried oregano, crushed
· ½ tsp. dried basil, crushed
· 12 tortillas
· 3 ½ c. shredded Monterey Jack cheese
· ¾ c. sour cream

Preheat oven to 350°.

Cut cooked chicken into strips. In a saucepan, cook onion and garlic in butter until tender. Add tomatoes, tomato sauce, chiles, sugar, cumin, salt, oregano, and basil. Bring to a boil, reduce heat, and simmer covered for 20 minutes. Remove from heat.

Dip tortilla in tomato sauce mixture to soften. Place one piece of chicken and about 2 Tbsp. cheese in the tortilla, roll up, and place in a casserole dish with seam-side down.

Blend sour cream with remaining sauce and pour over tortillas. Sprinkle with remaining cheese. Cover and bake at 350° for 40 minutes or until heated through.

Serves 6-8.

Low Fat Chicken Enchiladas

· 3 chicken breasts
· 2 c. water
· 1 Tbsp. chicken bouillon or 1 bouillon cube
· 1 bay leaf
· 1 tsp. red pepper flakes
· 1 yellow onion, chopped
· 1 c. celery, chopped
· 1 c. low fat cottage cheese
· 1 c. mozzarella cheese, shredded
· 1 green bell pepper, diced
· 1 can tomatoes with green chiles
· 1 Tbsp. chili powder
· 1 Tbsp. cumin
· 1 tsp. garlic powder
· 10-12 corn tortillas
· 2 (14 oz.) cans red or green enchilada sauce
· ½ c. cheddar cheese,
· ½ c. mozzarella or colby-jack cheese
· 1 c. cilantro, chopped
· Cooking spray
· Salt and pepper, to taste

Place first seven ingredients into pan and bring to boil. Let simmer for 30 minutes or until chicken is fully cooked. Drain excess water if needed and shred chicken and place in large bowl.

Combine cottage cheese, 1 cup mozzarella cheese, green pepper, tomatoes with chiles, and spices with the chicken mixture. Mix well then set aside.

Preheat oven to 350°. Spray sides of corn tortilla with cooking spray before placing on baking sheet in single layer. Place baking sheet in oven and warm tortillas until pliable or 3 to 5 minutes.

Spray casserole dish with cooking spray and spread ½ cup of enchilada sauce into the bottom of dish. Remove tortillas from oven and fill each tortilla with chicken and cheese mixture. Roll up and place each one side-by-side with seam-side down. Fill casserole dish and pour remainder of enchilada sauce on top of enchiladas, followed by the remaining cheeses and cilantro.

Place casserole dish into the oven for 30 to 45 minutes or until cheese is bubbly. Remove from oven and let cool 5 minutes before serving.

Serves 4-6.

Chicken Taco Stew

· 1 package boneless, skinless chicken breasts, cut into
    equal-size strips
· 2 qts. water
· 1 Tbsp. chopped onion
· 1 package low sodium taco seasoning
· 1 (28 oz.) can diced tomatoes and 1 (15 oz.) can tomato
    sauce for thinner stew, or use tomato paste for a thicker
    broth
· 1 (32 oz.) bag mixed frozen vegetables of your choice
· 1 (16 oz.) can black beans

Bring water to a rolling boil, add chicken and spices.
Reduce heat to medium and simmer covered for 45
minutes to 1 hour or until chicken is tender and the liquid
is reduced by half. Add tomatoes, mixed vegetables, and
black beans. Bring to a boil for 5 minutes then reduce
heat and simmer for 20 to 30 minutes until vegetables are
tender.

Serves 16.

White Bean and Chicken Chili

· 1 c. onion, chopped
· 1 garlic clove, minced
· ¼ c. butter
· 1 c. water (if too thick)
· 1 can chicken broth
· 3 cans northern white beans
· 2 cans pinto beans
· 1 Tbsp. fresh cilantro or additional if desired
· 1 Tbsp. dried basil
· 1 can tomatoes with chiles
· 1 small can diced green chiles
· 2 tsp. crushed red pepper
· 4 - 6 cooked chicken breasts, cubed

In a large stockpot, sauté onion and garlic in butter until
tender. Add remaining ingredients and simmer until
cooked through.

Garnish with your choice of tortillas, tortilla chips, sour
cream, shredded cheese, and jalapeños.

Serves 4.

Quick Creamed Chicken

· 1 Tbsp. butter
· ¼ c. green bell pepper, minced
· 1 (10 ¾ oz.) can cream of chicken or mushroom soup
· ¼ c. milk
· 2 c. cooked chicken or turkey, chopped
· 1 Tbsp. diced pimiento
· Parsley, paprika, or grated cheese for garnish

In hot butter, sauté green pepper until tender. Stir in soup and milk, then heat slowly. Add chicken and pimiento. Cook 10 to 15 minutes.

Pour into pastry shells, over English muffins, or cooked rice. Garnish with parsley, paprika, or grated cheese.

Serves 4-6.

Chicken Cutlets with Raisins, Pineapple, and Rum

· 12 chicken breasts; boned, tenderized, and skinless
· 1 c. chicken broth
· 1 c. orange juice
· 1 ½ c. purple raisins
· 1 ½ c. dark rum
· ¾ large can crushed unsweetened pineapple, reserve pineapple juice
· 5 tsp. cornstarch, dissolved in 4 Tbsp. water
· ½ tsp. garlic (optional)
· Toasted almonds
· Salt and pepper, to taste

Soak raisins in rum. Salt and pepper chicken, then brown in skillet. Set aside.

In a saucepan, mix the orange juice, broth, pineapple juice, raisins, rum, pineapple, and the dissolved cornstarch. Simmer until thickened, then add chicken to the sauce. Cook another five minutes to mix flavors. Sprinkle with toasted almonds.

Serves 12.

Chicken Saltimbocca

· 1 c. all-purpose flour
· Salt and pepper, to taste
· 4 (8 oz.) chicken breasts
· 4 large slices prosciutto
· 4 large fresh sage leaves, plus 20 smaller leaves
· 2 c. plus 4 Tbsp. extra-virgin olive oil
· 4 shallots, thinly sliced
· 1 lb. oyster mushrooms, sliced into ¼-inch pieces
· 1 c. Marsala wine
· ½ c. chicken stock
· 2 Tbsp. butter
· 1 bunch Italian parsley, chopped to yield ¼ cup

Season the flour with salt and pepper. With a meat mallet, pound the chicken breasts to ¼-inch thickness. Season each breast with salt and pepper and lay 1 sage leaf on each breast. Lay 1 slice prosciutto over each piece and fold in half like a book. Secure the two sides with a toothpick and dredge each breast in the seasoned flour.

In a heavy-bottomed pot with high sides, heat the 2 cups olive oil to 375°. Make sure that you have a slotted spoon or spider close by. Working in a few batches, fry the leaves in the oil, removing with the slotted spoon after 30 seconds. Season with salt, set on a plate lined with paper towels to drain, and set aside.

In a 12 to 14-inch sauté pan, heat the remaining olive oil until smoking. Add the chicken and sauté until golden brown on both sides. Add the shallots and mushrooms and cook until the mushrooms have sweated, about 5 to 6 minutes. Add the Marsala and chicken stock and cook over high heat until reduced by half. Swirl the butter into the pan, add the parsley and serve on 4 warmed dinner plates, topped with the fried sage leaves.

Serves 4-6.

Chicken Scampi

· 2 lb. chicken tenders, boneless and skinless
· 2 green bell peppers, sliced
· 2 red bell peppers, sliced
· 2 yellow bell peppers, sliced
· 1 medium yellow onion, sliced
· 2 to 3 cloves of garlic, crushed
· 1 - 2 Tbsp. olive oil
· 1 package angel hair pasta
· ½ c. flour
· 1 Tbsp. garlic powder
· 1 package Parma Rosa sauce mix or sauce mix of
    choice, prepared according to package directions

In a large skillet sauté peppers, onion, and garlic in olive oil on medium-low heat until tender or caramelized. Remove vegetables from skillet. Bread chicken in flour and cook on medium heat in skillet with olive oil until tender.

Cook pasta and toss pasta with olive oil, garlic powder, and salt and pepper. Serve chicken and vegetables over pasta and sauce.

Serves 4-6.

Victory Gymnastics' Hawaiian Chicken

· 3 lb. boneless and skinless chicken thighs
· 2 tsp. garlic powder
· ½ tsp. ginger
· 1 c. soy sauce
· 1 ½ c. sugar
· 1 c. ketchup
· ½ c. lemon juice
· 1 Tbsp. salt

Preheat oven to 350°.

Combine all ingredients except chicken thighs. Place chicken in large plastic zip bag and pour marinade over chicken. Seal bag and marinate overnight or freeze for later.

Place in 9x13-inch casserole dish and bake at 350° for 1 hour and 15 minutes, uncovered.

Serve over rice.

Serves 4-6.

Lemon Chicken

· 6 chicken breast halves, cut into equal pieces
· 2 Tbsp. flour
· 2 slices country ham steaks, diced
· 4 Tbsp. butter
· ½ c. chicken stock
· 2 Tbsp. lemon juice
· 2 Tbsp. chopped fresh parsley
· Salt and pepper, to taste

Combine flour, salt, and pepper. Dust chicken with flour mixture, reserving excess for sauce.

Melt butter in skillet and sauté ham and chicken. Remove from skillet and add remaining flour and chicken broth. Bring to a boil. Cook for 5 minutes, stirring until sauce thickens. Add lemon juice, parsley, ham, and chicken, stir to coat.

Serves 4-6.

Pork Entrées

Wine Pairings with Pork Entrées

Richer whites, like most Chardonnays and Pinot Blanc, go well with lighter meats like pork (as well as chicken and veal). A rich White Burgundy (Chardonnay) makes a natural match, or an Alsatian Riesling or Gewurztraminer; but a light red like Beaujolais or even a lighter-styled Pinot Noir is also fine.

Sausage Rigatoni

· 2 c. rigatoni
· 1 lb. ground sausage
· Basil, to taste
· Oregano, to taste
· Garlic powder, to taste
· Black pepper, to taste
· 4 c. spaghetti sauce
· 1-1 ½ c. sour cream
· 8 oz. Mozzarella cheese, sliced
· 8 oz. Provolone cheese, sliced
· ½-1 c. Parmesan cheese, shredded

Preheat oven to 350°.

Boil rigatoni in salted water until tender; drain.

Sauté sausage until brown; drain grease.

Assemble the following in a 2-qt. casserole dish: rigatoni, ½ of spaghetti sauce, Provolone cheese, sour cream, and meat, sprinkle seasonings over meat, then add Mozzarella cheese, and remaining spaghetti sauce. Finally top with Parmesan cheese.

Bake at 350° for 1 hour or until bubbly.

Bob Stoops' Sausage Stew

· 1 package Italian sausage links
· 2 (16 oz.) cans tomato sauce
· 1 (16 oz.) can stewed tomatoes
· 2 yellow bell peppers, sliced
· 2 red bell peppers, sliced
· 1 ½ white onions, chopped into chunks

Brown Italian sausage links. Layer browned sausages, tomato sauce, stewed tomatoes, peppers, and onions in a crock-pot. Cook on low for 4 to 6 hours.

Pour over hoagie buns or rigatoni and serve.

Carolina Barbecue Pulled Pork

· 2 onions, quartered
· 2 Tbsp. brown sugar
· 1 Tbsp. smoked paprika
· 2 tsp. salt
· ½ tsp. ground black pepper
· 1 (4-6 lb.) pork butt or shoulder roast
· 1 c. cider vinegar
· ⅓ c. Worcestershire sauce
· 1 ½ tsp. crushed red pepper flakes
· 2 tsp. sugar
· ½ tsp. dry mustard
· ½ tsp. garlic salt
· ½ tsp. cayenne pepper

Place onions in crock-pot. Blend brown sugar, paprika, salt and pepper; rub over roast. Place roast in crock-pot. Combine vinegar, Worcestershire sauce, red pepper flakes, sugar, mustard, garlic salt, and cayenne pepper and stir to mix well. Drizzle vinegar mixture over roast.

Cook roast on low for 8 to 10 hours. Remove meat and onions, discard onions and shred meat. Serve plain or as sandwiches.

Merlene's Pork Tenderloin

· 1-inch piece fresh ginger, peeled and grated
· 1-2 fresh jalapeños, deveined, seeded, and finely diced
· 1 Tbsp. crushed red pepper flakes
· ⅓ c. honey
· 3 Tbsp. soy sauce
· 3 Tbsp. sesame oil
· 2 lbs. (approximately) fresh pork tenderloin

Prepare and combine first six ingredients in small bowl. Place pork tenderloin in gallon-size plastic zip bag and pour marinade over meat. Rub outside of bag to make sure all of the meat is covered in the marinade. Marinate in refrigerator overnight for best results.

To cook pork, either grill or bake until internal temperature reaches 150-160°, but do not overcook. After removing from heat, allow pork to rest for 10 minutes before slicing.

Mother's Baked Ham

· 1 Ham
· ½ c. brown sugar
· 1 c. honey
· ¼ tsp. cloves
· 1 ½ tsp. cinnamon
· ½ tsp. ginger
· ½ tsp. dry mustard
· Salt and pepper, to taste
· 1 c. red or rosé wine
· 6 oz. lemon-lime soda

Preheat oven to 325°.

Combine all ingredients and pour over ham in baking dish. Bake at 325°, 20 minutes per pound.

Stuffed Ham Slices

· 4 Tbsp. butter, divided
· 1 large onion, chopped
· 1 tsp. prepared mustard
· ¾ c. herb-bread stuffing mix
· ½ - 1 c. chicken broth
· 6 large slices cold baked or boiled ham
· Parsley, chopped
· Salt and pepper, to taste

Preheat oven to 375°.

Heat 2 Tbsp. butter in a skillet; add onion and sauté until soft but not brown. Add the mustard, stuffing mix, and enough chicken broth to moisten and hold the mixture together. Season to taste with salt and pepper and spread on ham slices. Fold slices in half and secure with toothpick. Arrange in a flat, buttered baking dish. Melt the rest of the butter and brush over ham slices. Cover with foil and bake in a 375° oven for 30 minutes.

Garnish with parsley and serve.

Serves 6.

Pork Loin Roast with Plum Sauce

· 1 (2 ⅔ lbs.) boneless pork loin roast
· 2 cloves garlic, minced
· 1 tsp. ground sage
· ½ tsp. pepper

Plum Sauce
· ½ c. plum jam
· 1 ½ Tbsp. red wine vinegar
· 2 Tbsp. soy sauce
· ½ tsp. dry mustard
· ⅛ tsp. ground allspice

Preheat oven to 325°.

Combine garlic, sage, and pepper. Rub mixture over the entire roast. Place roast on a rack in a roasting pan. Insert meat thermometer into the thickest part of the roast and bake uncovered at 325° for approximately 2 hours or until the meat thermometer registers 170°.

Combine all the ingredients for the sauce in a small saucepan and bring to a boil. Reduce heat and cook for 2 minutes, stirring constantly. Spread a portion of the sauce over the roast during the last ½ hour of cooking. Serve remainder of the sauce at the table.

Pork Roast with Mushroom Sauce

· 2 lbs. lean pork roast, boned and well-formed for slicing, pork loin may be used

Mushroom Sauce
· 4 Tbsp. butter
· 4 Tbsp. flour
· ¼ tsp. salt
· ⅛ tsp. pepper
· 1 ¾ c. milk
· ½ lb. fresh mushrooms, sliced
· 2 Tbsp. lemon juice
· 4 Tbsp. butter
· ¼ lb. ground ham
· ¼ lb. Swiss cheese, grated
· Drippings from roast, fat removed

Preheat oven to 350°.

Salt and pepper roast; place on rack in roasting pan. Bake for 2 hours. Remove from oven and slice thin. Reserve drippings to add to sauce.

Melt butter. Blend in flour and seasonings. Stir in milk. Boil for 1 minute, stirring constantly. Sauté mushrooms in lemon juice and butter until just brown. Add mushrooms with liquid to sauce. Add ham, cheese, and drippings to white sauce. Return pork to baking dish, slice by slice, putting sauce between each slice. Cover with remaining sauce and bake for 30 minutes at 350° until bubbly.

Serve over rice.

Serves 8.

Sweet and Sour Pork

· 2 ½ - 3 lbs. pork roast
· Oil
· 2 small green bell peppers
· 1 medium onion
· 2 small tomatoes
· 1 ½ c. canned pineapple chunks
· ¾ c. vinegar
· ½ c. brown sugar
· 2 Tbsp. molasses
· 2 c. water
· 3 Tbsp. cornstarch

Cut pork roast into strips and brown in hot oil. Cut green peppers, onion, and tomatoes into strips.

When ready to eat, turn pork up to high and add vegetables and pineapple chunks.

Cook for a few minutes. Mix vinegar, brown sugar, molasses, and water in a separate bowl. Add vinegar mixture to pork and vegetables. Add cornstarch that has been mixed with a small amount of water; it will be the same consistency as soup. Add to pork and vegetables and stir until thickened.

Serve over rice.

Serves 8.

Big Ole Mess

· 1 lb. smoked sausage, cut into chunks
· 2 jalapeño peppers, sliced
· 1 green bell pepper, cut into bite-size chunks
· 1 sweet onion, cut into bite-size chunks
· ¼ c. Tabasco®
· 1 (10 oz.) jar sweet and sour sauce

Mix sausage, peppers, and onion in bowl. Mix Tabasco® and sweet and sour sauce in a small bowl and pour over the mixture.

To grill: Transfer to foil bag, sealing edge tightly. Grill foil bag for 45 minutes, turning every 15 minutes. Cut bag open and serve!

To bake: Transfer to glass baking dish, cover with foil, bake for 45 minutes at 400°.

Note – Can be served "sandwich style" on buns or crusty bread. Great on game days!

Oklahoma Memorial Union's
Roast Rack of Lamb

· 2 split racks of lamb, French-trimmed
· 2 cloves garlic, crushed
· ½ tsp. rosemary, de-stemmed
· Salt and pepper, to taste
· 12 oz. Mango Chutney (such as Major Grey's)
· 4 oz. honey
· 1 Tbsp. dry mustard
· 8 oz. dry roasted peanuts, chopped coarsely

Preheat oven to 350°.

Trim the rack of lamb. Wrap the ends of the ribs in aluminum foil to prevent burning. Rub rack thoroughly with garlic and rosemary. Season with salt and pepper to taste. Grill or sauté to sear and mark entire rack. Place in roasting pan and roast in 350° oven for 20 to 25 minutes for medium rare (brush with butter occasionally during roasting). Remove from oven and rest for 3 to 5 minutes.

Combine chutney, honey and dry mustard and coat rib side of rack heavily. Top with dry roasted peanuts. Set under broiler to heat chutney and brown peanuts.

Portion into 4 chops per person or 2 double chops per person.

Serves 4.

Beef Entrées

JAMES GARNER

Wine Pairings with Beef Entrées

Roast beef and steaks call for a dry, tannic red wine: Bordeaux or Cabernet Sauvignons and Merlots; Rhones or Syrah/Shiraz; and Northern Italian reds from Piemonte (Barolo, Barbaresco) to Tuscany (Chianti, Brunello).

Roast Beef Tenderloin with Mushrooms Bourguignon

· 4 lbs. filet of beef tenderloin (in two pieces)
· 2 tsp. salt
· ½ tsp. freshly ground black pepper
· 2 Tbsp. butter, softened

Mushrooms Bourguignon

· ⅓ c. butter
· 2 small green onions, chopped
· 1 clove garlic, crushed
· 1 lb. fresh mushrooms, sliced
· 1 c. Burgundy, or other red dinner wine
· ½ tsp. salt
· ⅛ tsp. freshly ground black pepper
· 2 Tbsp. parsley, chopped

For the beef: Preheat oven to 450°.

Sprinkle the filet pieces evenly with salt and pepper. Rub the softened butter on all sides of the meat. Insert a meat thermometer at least two inches into one end of the beef. Place the filet on a rack in a large, shallow pan. Roast in the middle of the oven for 30 minutes or until the thermometer reaches a temperature of 120°. Transfer the filet to a heated platter and let it rest at room temperature for 10 minutes before serving.

For the Mushrooms Bourguignon: Melt butter in a saucepan. Add the chopped onions, garlic, and mushrooms and sauté until tender. Add the red wine, salt, pepper, and parsley. Simmer until the wine is reduced in volume by half. The mushrooms will be quite dark. Serve over roast beef.

Legend's Filet of Beef with Green Madagascar Peppercorns

· 2 (8 oz.) tenderloin steaks
· Salt
· 2 Tbsp. butter
· 2 Tbsp. fresh shallots, minced
· 2 Tbsp. green Madagascar peppercorns
· ¼ c. red wine
· ½ c. brown sauce
· 1 Tbsp. fresh chopped parsley

Season the steaks with a little salt and cook to one degree short of the desired doneness, either by broiling, or by sautéing in a skillet with a small amount of the butter. Add the remaining butter to the skillet. Reduce the heat and add the shallots; simmer without browning. Add the green peppercorns, turning the steaks over in them. Add the red wine and deglaze the pan of any meat particles and sediment, using a scraper or rubber spatula to loosen these particles. Add the brown sauce and mix with the other ingredients and finally the chopped parsley. Correct the seasoning for salt, and pour the sauce over the steaks on the plates on which they will be served.

In the event you do not have brown sauce on hand, you may prepare an acceptable substitute using the following recipe:
· 2 Tbsp. cornstarch
· ¼ c. red wine
· 1 (10 ½ oz) can Campbell's® Beef Consommé Soup

Dissolve the cornstarch in the red wine, stir into the consommé, and heat over a high flame until the cornstarch has thickened, stirring constantly to prevent lumps.

Barbecued Beef Brisket

· 3 - 5 lb. brisket
· ½ bottle (3 ½ oz.) liquid smoke
· ⅛ tsp. garlic salt
· ¼ tsp. onion salt
· ¼ tsp. celery salt
· 3 Tbsp. Worcestershire sauce
· ⅛ tsp. salt
· ⅛ tsp. pepper
· ½ bottle barbecue sauce

Trim all excess fat from brisket. Combine liquid smoke, garlic salt, onion salt, and celery salt. Marinate brisket, covered in refrigerator, overnight or at least 8 hours.

Preheat oven to 250°.

Before cooking, sprinkle meat with Worcestershire sauce, salt and pepper. Cook tightly covered in oven at 250° for approximately 5 hours. Add ½ bottle barbecue sauce about the last half hour. Cool. Slice thinly across the grain.

Note – Good cold or hot.

Beef Tenderloin

· Beef tenderloin
· ¼ c. water
· 1 - 2 strips bacon
· ¼ stick butter, melted
· Salt and pepper, to taste

Preheat oven to 450°.

Cut as much fat off the tenderloin as possible. Place in a shallow pan; add ¼ cup water. Place bacon over the top of the tenderloin and pour melted butter over the top. Add salt and pepper. Bake uncovered at 450º for 30 minutes. Take out and let rest for 5 minutes before slicing.

Serve with a mixture of sour cream and horseradish on the side, to your taste.

Virge's Flank Steak

· 1 flank steak

Marinade:
· 4 Tbsp. oil
· 4 Tbsp. lemon juice
· 3 Tbsp. soy sauce
· 2 - 4 Tbsp. onion, chopped
· 1 tsp. Italian seasoning
· 4 - 6 dashes Tabasco® sauce

Marinate for 2 hours to 24 hours.

Slash the flank steak diagonally before cooking. Broil for 3 to 4 minutes on each side close to the heat. Slice thinly and serve.

Ricotta Meatloaf

Meatloaf
· 2 lbs. lean ground beef
· 2 eggs
· 1 lb. ricotta cheese
· Salt and pepper, to taste
· ⅓ -½ c. bread crumbs (optional)

Sauce
· 1 small onion, chopped
· 1 (16 oz.) can whole tomatoes
· ½ tsp. garlic powder
· ½ tsp. sugar
· ½ tsp. oregano
· 1 (8 oz.) can tomato paste
· 1 Tbsp. Worcestershire sauce
· Drops of hot sauce, to taste

Preheat oven to 350°.

Mix meatloaf ingredients.

For the sauce, sauté onions and add other ingredients; simmer about 20 minutes. Add about 1 cup sauce to meat/cheese mixture and form into a loaf. Add bread crumbs (about ⅓ –½ cup) if texture is wrong. Place in baking dish and put remaining sauce on the top. Bake at 350° for about 45 minutes.

Serves 10 - 12.

Ginger Beef

· ½ c. soy sauce
· ¼ c. water
· 2 Tbsp. sugar
· ¼ c. finely chopped onion
· 2 cloves garlic, crushed
· 2 tsp. ginger
· 1 ½ lbs. tenderized round steak, sliced into strips

Mix together all ingredients. Marinate meat for 2 hours in the refrigerator. Pan broil for 10 to 15 minutes until it gets a glazed look.

Serves 4-6.

Cabbage Rolls

· 1 c. rice, cooked
· 1 lb. ground beef
· 1 large can (28 oz.) tomatoes
· 1 tsp. salt
· ½ tsp. pepper
· ½ tsp. allspice
· 1 large head cabbage
· Juice of 2 lemons
· 3 large cloves garlic, sliced

Preheat oven to 350°.

Mix cooked rice, uncooked meat, and ½ can tomatoes. Add salt, pepper, and allspice. This is the filling.

Separate cabbage leaves and drop in salted boiling water, cooking separately until limp; then drain. Trim leaves of heavy stems and use stems to line the bottom of pan. If leaves are large, split in half.

Place 1 heaping Tbsp. of filling in leaf and roll firmly. Place rolls in pan making several layers; place garlic between layers. Add remaining tomatoes and enough hot water to cover rolls. Cook 45 minutes to 1 hour. During the last 15 minutes of cooking, add juice of 2 lemons.

Carne Asada

· 1 ½ - 2 lbs. flank steak or skirt steak

Marinade
· 2 ½ Tbsp. white vinegar
· ¼ c. soy sauce
· 3 garlic cloves, minced
· ½ tsp. garlic powder
· ½ tsp. chili powder
· ½ tsp. dried oregano
· ½ tsp. ground cumin
· ½ tsp. paprika
· Juice of 1 lime
· ¼ c. olive oil
· ⅓ c. orange juice
· 1 ½ Tbsp. ancho chile paste
· 1 tsp. salt
· 1 tsp. freshly ground black pepper

Combine ingredients for marinade and pour over the meat. Marinate, covered, in refrigerator overnight (the longer the better).

Grill or broil to desired doneness and let rest, covered, for at least 15 minutes before slicing thinly against the grain of the steak to insure tenderness.

Serve with tortillas and choice of toppings. Also great with rice, beans, sliced avocados, and a salad.

Steak Marinade

· ½ c. good quality coffee
· ¼ c. honey
· 2 Tbsp. oil
· 1 Tbsp. paprika
· 1 Tbsp. garlic salt
· ¼ tsp. ginger
· 1 lb. prime choice steak

Mix ingredients in a one gallon zip-top storage bag and add steak. Marinate overnight.

Note – Use flank steak for fajitas and substitute ¼ tsp. cumin for ginger.

Sweet and Smoky Rub

· 2 c. light brown sugar
· 2 Tbsp. paprika
· 2 Tbsp. chili powder
· 2 Tbsp. seasoned salt
· 1 Tbsp. garlic salt
· 1 Tbsp. lemon pepper
· 2 Tbsp. liquid smoke

Combine all ingredients into bowl; mix well. Spread out on cookie sheet to dry (2 to 3 hours). To use, rub into meat and refrigerate at least 2 hours.

Grill or cook as desired. Makes about 2 ½ cups of rub.

Note – Also great on pork, shellfish, or chicken!

Barry Switzer's Lasagna

· 1 lb. ground beef
· 1 medium onion, chopped
· 1 clove garlic, pressed
· 1 (16 oz.) can whole tomatoes
· 1 (15 oz.) can tomato sauce
· 2 Tbsp. parsley flakes
· 1 tsp. basil leaves
· 9 lasagna noodles
· 1 (16 oz.) carton Ricotta cheese
· ¼ c. grated Parmesan cheese
· 1 Tbsp. parsley flakes
· 1 ½ tsp. oregano leaves
· 2 c. shredded Mozzarella cheese
· ¼ c. grated Parmesan cheese

Preheat oven to 350°.

Cook and stir ground beef, onion, and garlic until meat is browned; drain. Add the next four ingredients and heat to boiling, stirring occasionally. Reduce heat and simmer uncovered for one hour until thick. Set aside ½ cup of sauce.

Cook lasagna noodles according to package directions. Mix Ricotta cheese and the next three ingredients. Divide sauce, noodles, Mozzarella cheese and cheese mixture. Beginning with three noodles, layer into a 13x9x2-inch pan. Repeat twice. Spoon reserved ½ cup of sauce on top and sprinkle with ¼ cup Parmesan cheese. Bake uncovered at 350° for 45 minutes.

Baked Spaghetti

· 1 c. canned diced tomatoes
· 2 c. tomato sauce
· 1 ½ tsp. sugar
· 1 c. water
· 2 small bay leaves
· 2 cloves garlic, minced
· ½ c. onion, diced
· 1 ½ lbs. ground beef
· ½ c. green bell pepper, diced
· 2 tsp. Italian seasoning
· ½ tsp. bell pepper
· 1 ½ tsp. seasoning salt
· 8 oz. uncooked angel-hair pasta
· 1 c. grated cheddar cheese, sharp
· ¼ c. fresh parsley, chopped
· 1 c. grated Monterey Jack cheese

Preheat oven to 350°.

Combine first six ingredients to make tomato sauce and simmer 1 hour, covered.

Cook meat, onion, and green bell pepper with Italian seasoning, pepper, and salt. Drain meat mixture; add to sauce and simmer 20 more minutes. Cook pasta and drain well. In a greased 9x13-inch pan, alternate layers of sauce, pasta, and cheddar cheese ending with sauce. Bake 30 minutes. Top with Monterey Jack cheese and bake 5 minutes more.

Garnish with fresh parsley and serve in squares.

Serves 10.

Spinach Bake

· 1 lb. lean ground beef
· 1 c. chopped onions
· 1 clove garlic, crushed
· 1 package (10 oz.) frozen chopped spinach, thawed
· 3 c. cooked rice
· 1 c. grated Monterey Jack cheese
· 4 eggs, beaten
· ¾ c. milk
· 1 tsp. salt
· ½ tsp. pepper
· 1 (15 oz.) can tomato sauce
· ½ tsp. each basil, oregano, and seasoned pepper
· 1 tsp. garlic salt
· ½ c. grated Parmesan cheese

Preheat oven to 350°.

Sauté beef, onions, and garlic until meat loses its red color. Add spinach, rice, and Monterey Jack cheese; mix well.

Combine eggs, milk, salt, and pepper. Stir into rice mixture. Pour into a lightly greased 9x13-inch baking dish. Bake at 350° for 30 minutes or until set.

While that mixture is baking, blend tomato sauce and seasonings. Simmer about 5 minutes.

Cut spinach mixture in squares and serve topped with tomato sauce and Parmesan cheese.

Serves 6.

Veal Parmesan

· ½ cup onion, chopped
· 1 Tbsp. oil
· 2 (8 oz.) cans of tomato sauce
· 1 clove garlic
· 2 tsp. oregano
· 1 bay leaf
· 1 egg
· ½ c. dry bread crumbs
· ½ c. Parmesan cheese, grated
· 6 veal cutlets
· ¼ c. cooking oil
· 6 oz. Mozzarella cheese, sliced
· ½ c. Parmesan cheese, grated

Preheat oven to 350°.

In saucepan, sauté onion in 1 Tbsp. of oil. Add tomato sauce, garlic, oregano, and bay leaf. Simmer 10 to 15 minutes. Remove bay leaf.

Beat egg in bowl. In separate bowl, combine bread crumbs and Parmesan cheese. Dip cutlets into egg then crumb mixture. Brown cutlets in ¼ cup of oil. Remove and drain on paper towels.

Place cutlets in 13×9×2-inch baking dish. Place half tomato sauce over cutlets. Top with Mozzarella cheese. Cover cheese with remaining tomato sauce and sprinkle ½ cup of Parmesan cheese over top. Bake for 45 minutes.

Serves 6-8.

Luciano's Veal Marsala

· 4 oz. veal scallops, thinly sliced
· Flour
· 4 Tbsp. butter
· 4 mushrooms, sliced
· ½ c. Marsala wine
· ½ c. cream
· Salt and pepper, to taste
· Fresh parsley, for garnish

Pound veal on both sides until thin. Lightly flour both sides of veal. Sauté each side on medium for 2 minutes. Discard the drippings.

Sauté mushrooms in fresh butter. Add Marsala wine, cream, salt and pepper to taste. Garnish with fresh parsley.

G.T. Blankenship's Oven Stew

· 2 lbs. beef stew meat
· 4 carrots, peeled, cut into chunks
· 1 onion, cut in chucks
· 4 pieces celery, cut in chucks
· 2 potatoes, peeled, cut in chucks
· 1 green bell pepper (optional), chopped
· 1 c. mushrooms (optional), chopped
· 1 large can diced tomatoes and juice
· ¼ c. minute tapioca
· ¼ c. bread crumbs
· ¼ c. red wine
· ½ tsp. salt
· ½ tsp. pepper

Preheat oven to 325°.

Place all ingredients into a Dutch oven and bake for 4 hours.

Amspacher's State Championship Chili

· 5 lbs. ground chuck
· 5 lbs. lean round steak, chili grind
· ¾ c. chili powder
· 1 Tbsp. of cumin
· 2 Tbsp. ground chili peppers
· 2 Tbsp. paprika
· 2 Tbsp. salt
· 1 Tbsp. crushed red peppers
· 2 (28 oz.) cans whole peeled tomatoes, or fresh
· 3 Tbsp. finely chopped fresh garlic
· 2 medium onions, chopped
· 4 fresh jalapeño peppers, chopped
· 12 oz. tomato juice

Brown meat in large pot. Do not drain. Add remaining ingredients. Simmer slowly for 3 hours. If needed, skim grease after chili has set for 2 hours.

Serves 25.

Olga's Chili

· 2 lbs. ground beef
· 1 can tomato soup
· 1 can pinto beans
· 1 can red kidney beans
· 1 can tomatoes
· 1 can chopped celery (use soup can for measuring)
· 1 can chopped onion
· 1 large garlic bud, minced
· ¼ tsp. salt
· ¼ tsp. pepper
· Chili powder, to taste (about 2 tsp.)
· Cheese and corn chips, as topping

Preheat oven to 325°.

Cook meat until the red is no longer visible. Pour off grease. Add all ingredients and bake at 325° for 2 ½ to 3 hours uncovered. Stir about every 30 minutes.

Serve with grated cheese and corn chips.

Serves 8.

Fish & Seafood Entrées

Wine Pairings with Fish & Seafood Entrées

If the fish itself has a lot of flavor (such as Tuna) or it is any kind of fish in a rich, buttery sauce, then pair with a full-flavored wine, such as a Chardonnay.

If the fish is naturally light in flavor or in a lemon sauce (such as Tilipia or Mahi Mahi) and the sauce does not change the characteristic, then pair with a lighter wine such as a Sauvignon Blanc.

Salmon has a richer, more distinct flavor than the average fish. So, it needs a wine with a richer, more developed flavor to go with it, such as a Pinot Noir or Burgundy.

"The" Famous Shrimp Boil and Butter Sauce

The Boil:
· 1 can of beer
· ½ tsp. thyme
· ½ tsp. dry mustard
· ½ tsp. chopped chives
· ½ tsp. salt
· ¼ tsp. pepper
· Bay leaf
· Clove of garlic
· 1 Tbsp. chopped parsley
· 1 lb. of shrimp, uncooked

Butter Sauce for 2
· 4 Tbsp. butter
· 2 Tbsp. lemon juice
· 1 tsp. chopped parsley
· 1 tsp. chopped chives
· 1 tsp. salt

For the Boil: Combine all ingredients, bringing to a boil. Continue boiling for 3 minutes.

For the Butter Sauce: Combine all ingredients; heat and serve with cooked shrimp.

Serves 2.

Creamy Shrimp and Rice

· 1 stick unsalted butter, room temperature
· 2 c. long grain rice
· 3 ½ c. chicken stock
· 2 tsp. sea salt
· 1 clove garlic, minced
· 2 lbs. small shrimp, peeled and deveined
· ½ c. lemon juice
· 1 tsp. hot sauce
· 1 c. whipping cream
· Freshly ground pepper

In medium saucepan, heat ½ of the butter on medium-low. Add rice and cook, stirring until golden. Add chicken stock and salt; bring to a boil. Reduce heat to medium-low and simmer 20 minutes (until rice is tender). Remove the pan from the heat and let rest.

In large skillet, melt remaining butter over medium heat. Add the garlic and cook for 1 to 2 minutes. Add shrimp, lemon juice, and hot sauce. Cook 2 to 3 minutes until shrimp is pink. Stir in the cream and heat through.

Season with salt and pepper to taste. Fluff the rice with a fork and spoon the shrimp cream sauce over the rice.

Garlic-Basil Shrimp

· 2 Tbsp. olive oil
· 1 ¼ lbs. large shrimp (20 - 25 per lb.),
   peeled and deveined
· 3 garlic cloves, minced
· ⅛ tsp. red pepper flakes, or more to taste
· ¾ c. dry white wine
· 1 ½ c. grape tomatoes, halved
· ¼ c. finely chopped fresh basil
· Salt and freshly ground black pepper, to taste
· 3 c. cooked orzo, preferably whole wheat

Heat the oil in a large, heavy skillet over medium-high heat until hot but not smoking. Add the shrimp and cook, turning over once, until just cooked through, about 2 minutes. Transfer with a slotted spoon to a large bowl.

Add the garlic and red pepper flakes to the oil remaining in the skillet and cook until fragrant, about 30 seconds. Add the wine and cook over high heat, stirring occasionally, for 3 minutes. Stir in the tomatoes and basil; season the sauce with salt and pepper. Return the shrimp to pan, and cook just until heated through.

Serve with the orzo.

Shrimp Victoria

· 1 c. cream sauce (recipe below)
· 1 lb. medium shrimp, cleaned and deveined
· 4 Tbsp. butter, divided
· ½ c. mushrooms, sliced
· 3 - 4 green onions, finely chopped
· ½ c. dry white wine
· ½ c. sour cream
· 1 Tbsp. parsley
· 1 pinch thyme

Cream Sauce
· 4 Tbsp. butter
· ¾ c. milk, heated
· ⅛ tsp. cayenne, or to taste
· ¼ c. flour
· ⅓ tsp. salt

Melt butter and stir in flour; blend well without browning. Add milk. Season with salt and cayenne. Stir constantly until thick.

Prepare cream sauce. Sauté shrimp lightly in 2 Tbsp. butter. Sauté onions and mushrooms in 2 Tbsp. butter. Add wine and blend. Gradually blend in cream sauce. Add shrimp. Blend in sour cream, parsley, and thyme. Do not boil.

Serve over rice.

Serves 4.

Seafood Alfredo

· 2 tsp. crushed garlic
· 2 Tbsp. vegetable oil
· 1 stick butter, divided
· 6 medium sea scallops, cut into quarters
· 1 lb. medium shrimp, cleaned, deveined, and cut in half
· ½ lb. lump crabmeat, or two small lobster
     tails, cut into small pieces
· 2 c. heavy cream
· 2 c. shredded Mozzarella cheese
· 2 c. shredded Parmesan cheese
· 1 loaf of whole garlic clove bread or
     other crusty loaf, sliced thin
· 1 lb. angel hair pasta

In medium skillet, heat oil and half stick butter until hot. Sauté garlic for two minutes. Add seafood and sauté for 4 or 5 minutes; remove from heat and oil.

Cook pasta to desired tenderness. Drain well.

Heat cream, but don't boil. When hot, add cheeses and stir until completely melted into sauce. Add drained seafood to sauce mixture. Toss with cooked pasta.

Melt other half stick of butter and brush onto bread slices. Toast bread until starting to brown, and serve on the side.

Serves 4.

White Clam Spaghetti Sauce

· 4 (7 oz.) cans minced clams, undrained
· 2 sticks butter or margarine
· 5 cloves garlic, smashed
· ½ tsp. garlic salt
· 1 Tbsp. lemon juice
· 1 Tbsp. onion, grated
· 1 tsp. chopped parsley
· 1 tsp. chives
· ½ tsp. white pepper
· ½ pt. heavy cream
· 1 Tbsp. cornstarch
· 16 oz. spaghetti

Pour clams and juice into saucepan. Add butter and melt. Add next seven ingredients and simmer 15 minutes. Combine heavy cream and cornstarch. Add to sauce. Do not allow to get too thick. Thicken just enough to keep it on the spaghetti.

Cook spaghetti according to package directions and toss with sauce.

Serves 6-8.

Crab Enchiladas

· 2 (8 oz.) packages cream cheese, softened
· 6 green onions, chopped
· 1 lb. crabmeat, fresh or frozen
· 2 (10 oz.) cans tomatillos, use fresh if available
    peeling paper-like covering first and chop
· 1 (4 oz.) can whole green chiles, rinsed and drained
· 6 small sprigs cilantro, chopped
· 2 c. heavy cream
· 3 green onions, chopped
· 2 eggs, beaten
· ¾ avocado
· Garlic salt to taste
· 1 dozen flour tortillas
· Sour cream and avocado slices, for garnish

Preheat oven to 350°.

Combine cream cheese, 6 green onions, and crabmeat. Refrigerate until ready to stuff tortillas.

In blender, combine tomatillos with green chiles, and cilantro. Blend until smooth. Add cream, eggs, 3 chopped green onions, avocado, and garlic salt. Blend again. Pour in saucepan and warm over low heat. Soften tortillas in hot oil.

Drain tortillas and blot excess oil. Stuff tortillas with crab mix and roll. Pour sauce over tortillas. Heat in 350° oven for 30 minutes.

Garnish with sour cream and avocado slices.

Serves 6.

Heart-Healthy Salmon with Lemon Basil Spaghetti

· ½ lb. whole-wheat spaghetti pasta
· 2 clove garlic, minced
· 2 Tbsp. extra-virgin olive oil
· ½ tsp. salt, plus more for seasoning
· ½ tsp. freshly ground black pepper,
    plus more for seasoning
· 1 Tbsp. olive oil
· 4 (4 oz.) pieces salmon
· ¼ c. chopped fresh basil leaves
· 4 Tbsp. capers
· 1 lemon, zested
· 2 Tbsp. lemon juice
· 2 ½ c. fresh baby spinach leaves or arugula

Bring a large pot of salted water to a boil over high heat. Add the pasta and cook until tender but still firm to the bite, stirring occasionally, about 8 to 10 minutes. Drain pasta and transfer to a large bowl. Add the garlic, extra-virgin olive oil, salt, and pepper. Toss to combine.

Meanwhile, warm the olive oil in a medium skillet over medium-high heat. Season the salmon with salt and pepper. Add the fish to the pan and cook until medium-rare, about 2 minutes per side, depending on the thickness of the fish. Remove the salmon from the pan.

Add the basil, capers, lemon zest, and lemon juice to the spaghetti mixture and toss to combine.

Slightly wilt spinach leaves in hot pan for approximately 2 minutes. Place spinach on plate or bowl and top with the pasta. Top each mound of pasta with a piece of salmon. Serve immediately.

Serves 4.

Black Bean Salmon

· 2 Tbsp. black bean sauce
· 2 Tbsp. miso paste (any color miso is fine)
· 2 scallions, white and most of the green,
    thinly sliced on the diagonal
· 2 tsp. minced fresh ginger
· ¼ tsp. freshly ground black pepper
· 1 tsp. toasted sesame oil
· 1 ½ lbs. wild salmon, cut into four 6 oz. portions (can
    substitute farm raised if wild is unavailable)

Preheat oven to 375°.

In a small bowl, mix the black bean sauce with the miso,
scallions, ginger, pepper, and sesame oil. Rub the mixture
over each piece of salmon; place on a baking sheet lined
with parchment paper or foil. Bake for 10 to 12 minutes.

Serve hot.

Serves 4.

Fish-n-Chips

· 2 lbs. fish fillets
· ¼ c. lemon juice
· 2 Tbsp. Italian salad dressing
· 2 c. crushed potato chips
· ½ c. grated Parmesan cheese
· ¼ c. chopped parsley
· 1 ½ tsp. paprika
· ½ tsp. thyme
· Lemon wedges, for garnish

Preheat oven to 500°.

Combine lemon juice and salad dressing.

Combine potato chips, cheese, parsley, and seasonings. Dip
fish in lemon juice mixture and roll in chip mixture. Place
fish on a well-greased cookie sheet. Bake at 500° for 10 to 15
minutes, until fish flakes with fork.

Serve with lemon wedges.

Serves 6-8.

Low-Fat Blackened Fish Tacos

Slaw
· ¼ c. sliced green onions with tops
· 3 Tbsp. snipped fresh cilantro
· 1 Tbsp. fresh lime juice
· 1 Tbsp. Olive oil
· 2 garlic cloves, pressed
· 1 tsp. sugar
· 2 tsp. blackened seasoning
· 2 c. broccoli slaw mix

Fish
· 2 filets of Mahi-Mahi (can also use Tilapia)
· 1 Tbsp. blackened seasoning
· 1 Avocado, seeded and sliced
· 8 corn tortillas, warmed
· 3 medium radishes
· Additional snipped fresh cilantro for topping

For the Slaw: combine green onions, cilantro, lime juice, olive oil, garlic, sugar, and blackened seasoning: whisk until blended. Add slaw mix; toss to coat. Cover; refrigerate until ready to serve.

For the Fish: Heat grill pan or outdoor grill over medium heat. Moisten fish fillets with water and sprinkle with blackened seasoning. Spray pan with cooking spray or olive oil. Place fillets in pan; cook over medium heat 10 to 12 minutes or until fish flakes with fork, carefully turning once. Remove from heat. Flake fish into bite-size pieces.

Top tortillas evenly with slaw mixture and fish. Grate radishes over fish, top with avocado slices, and sprinkle with additional cilantro.

Serves 4.

Sole with Mushroom Sauce

· 6 fillets of sole (1 ½ lbs.)
· 1 tsp. salt
· ¼ tsp. white pepper
· 3 Tbsp. butter
· ¾ c. onions, finely chopped
· ¼ lb. mushrooms, thinly sliced
· ½ c. dry white wine
· 1 Tbsp. flour
· ½ c. milk
· 1 Tbsp. parsley, minced

Wash and dry the fillets; season with salt and pepper.

Melt butter in a large skillet; add onions and sauté about 5 minutes. Arrange the fillets in the skillet and cover with mushrooms. Add the wine and cover. Cook over medium heat for 15 minutes or until fish flakes easily when tested with a fork. Transfer fish to a heated serving dish and keep warm.

Mix together the flour and milk; add to the skillet, mixing steadily until it boils. Cook over low heat for 5 minutes. Pour over the fish and sprinkle with parsley.

Serves 6.

Catfish Fillets

· 2 ¼ lbs. catfish fillets
· 1 lb. yellow cornmeal

Marinade
· 1 part Louisiana Hot Sauce®
· ½ part water
· Salt and pepper, to taste
· ½ tsp. celery seed
· 1 tsp. dill weed
· ½ Tbsp. onion powder
· ½ tsp. garlic powder
· ¼ tsp. cayenne pepper
· 1 Tbsp. lemon pepper

Heat oil to 380° using a thermometer.

Wash and pat dry fish fillets then place in the marinade. After fish have marinated, roll in cornmeal. Cook 3 or 4 minutes. Do not cook too many pieces at one time so temperature of oil will not drop below 360°. Do not let oil rise above 395°. Fish will float, steam, and bubbles will calm down. Fish will continue cooking after removing from oil. If fish flesh is white and shiny with moisture, it is done.

Serves 7-10.

Side Dishes

Cheesy Spinach Puff

· ½ c. butter
· 3 Tbsp. flour
· 1 (10 oz.) package frozen spinach, thawed and drained
· 3 eggs, beaten
· ¾ c. milk
· 1 c. cheddar cheese, grated

Preheat oven to 350°.

Melt butter and stir in flour. Add spinach, eggs, and milk. Add ½ cup of cheese. Pour into buttered 1-quart soufflé dish. Top with remaining ½ cup of cheese. Bake at 350° for 45 minutes.

Chili-Roasted Sweet Potatoes

· 4 medium sweet potatoes
· 2 Tbsp. olive oil
· 1 tsp. chili powder
· Kosher salt and fresh ground pepper, to taste

Preheat oven to 450°.

Peel sweet potatoes and cut into equal-size pieces. Toss the potatoes in a large bowl with olive oil, chili powder, salt, and pepper until all sides are coated. Spread on a baking sheet and bake 25 minutes or until done, turning them over halfway through the cooking time.

Serves 4-6.

Fried Green Tomatoes

· 2 lbs. green tomatoes cut into ¼-inch slices
· ½ c. breadcrumbs
· ½ c. cornmeal
· 1 c. flour
· 4 eggs
· 1 c. vegetable oil
· Garlic salt, to taste
· Salt and pepper, to taste

Pour oil into iron skillet and heat on medium-high.

Break eggs into a bowl and stir with fork. Combine the cornmeal and breadcrumbs in a separate bowl. Pour flour in a third bowl. Cut tomatoes into slices. Coat with flour then dip in egg wash. Lastly, dip into cornmeal/breadcrumb mixture.

Cook 4 to 5 minutes on each side until golden brown. Transfer to plate lined with paper towels, sprinkle with garlic salt, salt and pepper.

Serves 12.

Green Beans and Corn with Lime Sauce

· 16 oz. fresh or frozen green beans
· 8 oz. fresh, frozen, or canned corn kernels
· 1 lime, zest and juice
· 2 Tbsp. butter, melted
· Kosher salt and fresh ground pepper, to taste

Steam beans and corn, or warm according to package instructions. Zest and juice lime and add to melted butter. Just before serving, combine corn, beans, and butter mixture in a bowl and toss. Sprinkle with kosher salt and cracked pepper.

Serves 4-6.

Green Beans and Shallots

· 16 oz. fresh or frozen green beans
· 2 Tbsp. olive oil
· 2 finely chopped shallots (or white onions)
· Kosher salt and fresh pepper, to taste

Steam green beans to tender-crisp, or prepare according to package directions.

Sauté shallot or onion over medium heat until translucent.

In a large bowl, toss green beans and shallots together and sprinkle with kosher salt and cracked pepper.

Serves 4-6.

Holiday Cauliflower

· 1 large head of cauliflower
· 1 ½ lbs. fresh mushrooms, sliced
· ¼ c. green bell pepper, diced
· ¼ c. butter
· ⅓ c. flour
· 2 c. milk
· 1 tsp. salt
· 1 c. Swiss cheese, shredded
· 2 Tbsp. chopped pimiento

Preheat oven to 325°.

Break cauliflower into medium size florets and cook in boiling water until tender, about 10 minutes. Drain well, set aside.

In 2-quart saucepan, sauté mushrooms and green bell pepper in butter until tender. Blend in flour. Gradually stir in milk. Cook, stirring constantly, over medium heat until mixture thickens. Add salt, cheese, and pimiento.

Place half of cauliflower in buttered 2-quart casserole. Cover with half of sauce, repeat. Bake at 325° for 15 minutes.

Serves 8.

Marinated Green Beans

· 1 stick butter
· ½ c. brown sugar
· 1 Tbsp. soy sauce
· 1 clove garlic, pressed
· 3 large cans (28 oz.) greens beans, drained
· 8 slices of pepper bacon, chopped

Preheat oven to 350°.

Place green beans in 9×13-inch casserole dish. In small saucepan, bring the first four ingredients to a boil. Pour mixture over green beans and marinate overnight.

Before baking, cut eight slices of pepper bacon into pieces and sprinkle on top of green beans. Bake at 350° for 45 minutes to 1 hour or until bacon is cooked.

Oregon Walnut Broccoli

· 4 c. (1 ½ bunches) fresh broccoli, blanched and cut into florets
· ½ c. + 3 Tbsp. butter (divided)
· 4 Tbsp. flour
· 4 c. chicken broth
· ⅓ package dry stuffing mix
· ⅓ c. walnuts, chopped

Preheat oven to 350°.

Cook broccoli until tender. Drain and place in greased 9×13-inch casserole dish. In saucepan, over medium heat, melt ½ C. butter. Stir in flour until blended and add broth. Cook until thickened and pour over broccoli.

Melt remaining 3 Tbsp. butter and pour over stuffing mix. Toss to coat and layer over broccoli. Sprinkle with walnuts. Bake for 30 minutes.

Serves 6-8.

Sautéed Green Beans

· 3 c. green beans
· 1 Tbsp. olive oil
· 1 tsp. sesame seeds

Sauté green beans in olive oil until slightly tender. Sprinkle with sesame seeds and serve.

Serves 2-3.

The Admiral's Broccoli

· 2 packages frozen chopped broccoli
· 1 can mushroom soup
· 2 eggs, beaten
· 1 onion, minced
· 1 c. mayonnaise
· Salt and pepper, to taste
· 1 c. grated sharp cheddar cheese
· Butter for dish

Preheat oven to 325°.

Thaw and drain broccoli; place in a buttered 2-quart baking dish.

Mix soup, eggs, onion, mayonnaise, salt, and pepper. Pour over broccoli. Top with grated cheese. Bake at 325° for 45 minutes.

Serves 4.

Pennsylvania Dutch-Style Green Beans

· 3 strips bacon
· 1 small onion, sliced
· 2 tsp. cornstarch
· ¼ tsp. salt
· ¼ tsp. dry mustard
· 1 (16 oz.) can green beans
· 1 Tbsp. brown sugar
· 1 Tbsp. vinegar
· 1 hard-boiled egg, sliced

Fry bacon until crisp. Remove bacon and crumble. Drain all but 1 Tbsp. drippings. Add onion and brown lightly.

Stir in cornstarch, salt, and dry mustard. Drain beans, reserving ½ cup liquid. Stir reserved liquid into skillet. Cook, stirring until mixture boils. Blend in brown sugar and vinegar. Add green beans and heat thoroughly.

Garnish with egg and crumbled bacon.

Serves 4.

Mimmy's Squash

· 2 lbs. yellow squash
· 1 large onion, chopped
· 8-10 saltine crackers, crumbled or crushed
· Pinch of sugar
· Salt and pepper, to taste
· Scant ½ c. milk

Preheat oven to 350°.

Wash and peel toughest parts of squash. Parboil about 5 minutes. Drain well.

Sauté onion, preferably in bacon drippings. Mix onion and squash together. Layer in greased casserole with crumbled cracker crumbs, adding sugar, salt and pepper. Add milk about halfway up the squash.

Bake at 350° until bubbly.

Sautéed Spinach

· 1 bunch spinach, washed thoroughly and drain well
· 2 cloves garlic, pressed
· ¼ c. onions, diced
· 1 Tbsp. olive oil

Sauté garlic and onions in olive oil for 5 minutes. Add spinach and sauté for an additional 2 minutes, or until slightly limp. Serve immediately.

Scrumptious Zucchini

· 4-5 medium zucchinis, unpeeled and
    sliced in ¼-inch slices
· 3 medium carrots, shredded
· 1 medium onion, chopped
· 3 Tbsp. butter
· 1 can cream of chicken soup
· 1 c. sour cream
· 1 c. seasoned croutons

Preheat oven to 350°.

Boil zucchini until tender (about 5 to 7 minutes). Drain.

Meanwhile, sauté carrots and onion in 2 Tbsp. butter until limp. Mix soup and sour cream, add to vegetables. Add ¾ cup of the croutons and zucchini, stirring gently. Pour into greased 9x13-inch pan.

Combine remaining croutons and 1 Tbsp. of butter; heat until coated. Sprinkle on top of casserole. Bake at 350° for 20 to 25 minutes.

Serves 8.

Carrot Puff

· 1 lb. carrots, peeled and cut into 1-inch pieces
· 1 stick of butter
· 3 eggs
· ½ c. sugar
· 3 Tbsp. all-purpose flour
· 1 tsp. baking powder
· 1 tsp. vanilla

Preheat oven to 350°.

Place carrots in a medium-size saucepan and cover with water. Add salt, bring to a boil, reduce heat, and simmer 20 minutes or until the carrots are tender. Drain.

Place the melted butter, eggs, sugar, flour, baking powder, and vanilla in blender and puree. Add carrots a little at a time and puree the mixture. Pour into a greased 8-inch square baking dish.

Bake at 350° for 45 minutes or until firm. Let stand 5 minutes before serving.

Note – This can be prepared a day ahead and refrigerated. Bring to room temperature before baking.

Green Beans

· 1 ¼ lbs. fresh green beans
· 3 cloves garlic, minced
· 1 ½ c. Parmesan cheese, finely grated
· 1 Tbsp. Extra-virgin olive oil
· ½ Lemon, zested and juiced

Add the green beans to a pot of boiling, salted water; cook about 6 minutes. Drain the green beans, reserving the cooking liquid.

Put the pan back on the heat and add oil and garlic, then stir. When the garlic begins to brown, add the green beans, stirring to coat with oil. Add a ladle of reserved cooking liquid, the Parmesan cheese, and zest from the lemon. Next, add the lemon juice. Stir and simmer for a few minutes until the cheese melts.

Remove from heat and serve immediately.

Spicy Cabbage

· 2 tsp. dark sesame oil
· 1 tsp. chili oil
· ½ c. sliced onion
· 1 Tbsp. minced fresh ginger
· 1 tsp. minced garlic
· 1 red bell pepper, sliced thinly
· 1 green bell pepper, sliced thinly
· ½ c. julienne cut snow peas
· 1 medium head Napa cabbage, cored
    and cut crosswise into strips
· ¼ c. apple juice
· ¼ tsp. salt
· ¼ tsp. cayenne pepper
· 1 c. carrots, shredded
· 2 tsp. rice vinegar

Heat oils in nonstick skillet over medium-high heat. Add onion, ginger, bell peppers, and snow peas; stir-fry 1 minute. Add cabbage, apple juice, salt and cayenne. Cook 3 to 5 minutes or until cabbage is crisp-tender. Stir in carrot and vinegar. Serve immediately.

Squash and/or Zucchini Casserole

· 2 lbs. yellow squash or mix with zucchini
· 1 tsp. salt
· ⅛ tsp. sugar
· ½ stick butter
· 1 c. sour cream
· ½ c. onion, chopped
· ¼ c. white wine
· 1 ¼ c. sharp cheddar cheese, shredded
· ⅓ c. Parmesan cheese
· Buttered bread crumbs, for topping

Preheat oven to 350°.

Parboil squash with salt and sugar; drain well. Add butter and mash coarsely. Add remaining ingredients and mix together. Top with buttered crumbs. Bake 20 to 30 minutes.

Baked Vegetables

· 1 lb. vegetables of choice
· 1 onion, chopped
· 1 c. celery, chopped
· 1 stick butter
· 1 c. mayonnaise
· 1 sleeve butter crackers
· 1 c. shredded cheddar cheese

Preheat oven to 350°.

Steam vegetables about 5 minutes then place in 9×12-inch pan. Combine butter and mayonnaise and spread over vegetables. Crumble crackers over the top of mixture and sprinkle with cheese.

Bake at 350° for 45 minutes.

Serves 8-10.

Broccoli with Poppyseed Sauce

· 2 Tbsp. onion, chopped
· 2 Tbsp. butter
· 2 tsp. vinegar
· 2 tsp. sugar
· 1 tsp. poppy seeds
· 1 tsp. paprika
· Salt and pepper, to taste
· Dash cayenne pepper
· 1 ½ c. sour cream
· 2 bunches fresh broccoli, trimmed and stalks separated
· ¼ c. pecans, chopped (optional)

Sauté onion in butter until tender. Add vinegar, sugar, poppy seeds, paprika, salt, and cayenne pepper. Add sour cream. Heat thoroughly, but do not boil.

Steam broccoli, covered in boiling salted water, for approximately 10 to 15 minutes. Arrange freshly steamed broccoli on a serving dish. Pour sauce over broccoli and sprinkle with pecans.

Serves 6-7.

Goodie Corn Casserole

· 1 can whole corn
· 1 can cream style corn, juice only
· 1 c. sour cream
· 1 stick margarine, melted
· 1 (8 ½ oz.) box corn muffin mix
· Cooking spray

Preheat oven to 400°. Spray 9×13-inch pan with cooking spray.

Mix all ingredients together and pour into pan. Bake 35 to 40 minutes or until done.

Jiffy Corn Casserole

· 1 can whole kernel corn, undrained
· 1 can cream-style corn
· 1 c. sour cream
· ¼ c. sugar
· 2 eggs, beaten
· ½ c. melted butter
· 1 (8 oz.) package Jiffy® corn muffin mix

Preheat oven to 350°.

Mix all ingredients together, adding muffin mix last. Bake in a 9×13-inch casserole dish at 350° for 50 to 60 minutes until set. Let stand 5 minutes before serving.

Pastel de Elote (Corn Pie)

· 1 c. butter, softened
· ½ c. sugar
· 4 eggs
· 1 can (4 oz.) green chiles, drained and chopped
· 1 can cream-style corn
· ½ c. Monterey Jack cheese, shredded
· ½ c. cheddar cheese, shredded
· 1 c. all-purpose flour
· 1 c. yellow cornmeal
· 4 tsp. baking powder
· ¼ tsp. salt

Preheat oven to 350°.

Cream butter and sugar. Add eggs, chiles, corn, and cheese. Mix well.

Combine flour, cornmeal, baking powder, and salt; add to corn mixture. Pour into greased and floured baking dish (9×12-inch). Place dish in oven and reduce heat to 300°. Bake for 1 hour.

Serves 10-12.

BBQ Beans

· 1 (15 oz.) can pork and beans
· 1 (15 oz.) can pink beans, rinsed and drained
· 1 (15 oz.) can kidney beans, rinsed and drained
· ½ lb. bacon, cooked and chopped
· 2 c. smoked ham, chopped
· 1 large green bell pepper, chopped
· 1 large yellow onion, chopped
· 1 small green chile pepper, chopped
· 1 c. light brown sugar
· ½ c. barbeque sauce
· 2 cloves garlic, chopped

Preheat oven to 350°.

Combine all ingredients in 9x13-inch baking dish and cover with foil. Bake for 1 hour until bubbly.

Parsley Potatoes

· 3-5 red potatoes
· 2 Tbsp. parsley
· 1 Tbsp. butter
· Salt and pepper, to taste

Slice potatoes into even bite-size pieces. Boil until tender and drain. Add butter, salt, pepper, and parsley. Toss until blended.

Hash Brown Potato Casserole

· 1 (32 oz.) package shredded frozen potatoes
· 1 can cream of chicken soup, undiluted
· 12 oz. American cheese, grated
· 8 oz. sour cream
· 1 tsp. salt
· ½ small onion, chopped
· 2 c. cornflakes, crushed
· ½ c. melted butter

Preheat oven to 350°.

Place thawed potatoes in 9×13-inch baking dish. Mix together soup, cheese, sour cream, salt, and onion. Pour over potatoes. Top with crushed cornflakes. Drizzle melted butter over all. Bake uncovered at 350° for 45 minutes.

Serves 12.

Mashed Potato Casserole

· 8-10 potatoes, peeled and cubed
· 8 oz. sour cream
· 8 oz. cream cheese, softened
· ¼ c. chopped chives, more or less to taste
· Garlic salt, to taste
· Black pepper, to taste
· ¼ c. butter

Preheat oven to 350°.

Boil potatoes until tender. Drain and cool slightly. Place in large mixing bowl. Use electric mixer to "mash" to creamy texture. Mix in sour cream and cream cheese until smooth. Stir in chives, garlic salt, and black pepper. Put mixture into casserole dish. Dot the top of potatoes with butter. Bake at 350° for 45 minutes uncovered.

Note – Can be prepared ahead and refrigerated until ready to bake.

Dick Reynolds' Favorite New Potato Salad

· 2 ½ lbs. small, red new potatoes, washed and unpeeled
· 2 medium scallions, trimmed, cut into 1-inch pieces
· ¼ c. fresh dill
· Mustard Vinaigrette (recipe below)
· Salt and freshly ground black pepper, to taste
· 1 c. sour cream

Mustard Vinaigrette
· 1 ¼ c. wine vinegar
· 1 Tbsp. Dijon mustard
· 1 tsp. salt
· Freshly ground black pepper, to taste
· 1 c. olive oil

Cook the potatoes in boiling, salted water until just tender. Meanwhile, in a blender or food processor, process the scallion pieces and dill until finely chopped; reserve.

Drain the potatoes in a colander, and refresh them under cold running water. Cut them in half as soon as they can be handled and place in a large mixing bowl.

To make the mustard vinaigrette, process all ingredients in blender or food processor, except the oil, until combined, about 5 seconds. With the motor running, pour the oil in a slow, steady stream until incorporated. Pour the mustard vinaigrette over the potatoes, add the reserved scallion-dill mixture, and toss gently. Add salt and pepper to taste. Fold in the sour cream and let stand for at least 30 minutes before serving.

Oven Roasted Potatoes

· ⅛ c. olive oil
· 1 Tbsp. garlic, minced
· ½ tsp. dried basil
· ½ tsp. dried marjoram
· ½ tsp. dried dill weed
· ½ tsp. dried thyme
· ½ tsp. dried oregano
· ½ tsp. dried parsley
· ½ tsp. crushed red pepper flakes
· ½ tsp. salt
· 4 large potatoes, peeled and cubed

Preheat oven to 475°.

In a large bowl, combine oil, garlic, basil, marjoram, dill weed, thyme, oregano, parsley, red pepper flakes, and salt. Stir in potatoes until evenly coated.

Place potatoes in single layer on a roasting pan or baking sheet. Roast for 20 to 30 minutes turning occasionally to brown on all sides.

Heart-Healthy "Bubble & Squeak" (British Cabbage & Mashed Potatoes)

· 1 ½ lbs. potatoes, unpeeled and cut into chunks
· 1 c. warm low-fat milk
· 2 Tbsp. butter
· Pinch of nutmeg
· Salt and pepper, to taste
· 2 tsp. oil
· 1 head green cabbage, chopped
· 1 oz. lean ham, diced
· 1 onion, diced

Cook the potatoes in a pan of boiling water for 15 to 20 minutes. Once cooked through, drain and mash with potato masher. Add milk (more if dry), butter, nutmeg, and salt and pepper to taste. Set aside.

Heat oil in a very large nonstick pan over medium heat and add diced ham and onion. Cook until the ham is browned and the onions are translucent. Add cabbage to pan; cook until cabbage is slightly crunchy. Add salt and pepper to taste, and serve with the mashed potatoes on top.

Herb Butter Potatoes

· 2 large baking potatoes, peeled
· 1 medium white onion, diced
· 1 tsp. garlic (1 average-sized clove), minced
· ¼ tsp. each of salt and pepper
· Foil

Herb Butter
· ¼ c. butter
· 1 Tbsp. fresh chives, chopped
· 1 Tbsp. fresh parsley, chopped

Preheat oven to 375°.

Grease sheet of foil on cookie sheet. Melt butter and stir in chives and parsley; set aside.

Peel baking potatoes, cut into equal size pieces, and place on foil. Spread diced onions and minced garlic evenly over potatoes. Pour melted butter over potato mixture and season with salt and pepper. Cover with foil and seal tightly. Place in oven and cook for 45 to 60 minutes or until potatoes are tender.

Joan's Layered Potatoes

· 8 white Russet potatoes, washed and unpeeled
· 1 stick of margarine
· 2 white onions, sliced
· Sea salt, to taste
· Freshly ground pepper, to taste

Preheat oven to 450°.

Slice unpeeled white Russet potatoes and place in a layer over the bottom of a baking dish. Put sliced onion rings and pats of margarine on top; season with salt and pepper. Continue to layer (3 layers total) the ingredients. Cover with foil and cook in 450° oven until tender.

Shrimp Fried Rice

· ¼ to ½ c. oil
· ½ c. green bell pepper strips
· 1 c. celery, sliced slanted
· ½ c. chopped onion
· 1 Tbsp. soy sauce
· ½ c. bean sprouts
· 1 can water chestnuts, drained
· 3 c. cooked rice
· 4 to 5 oz. cooked shrimp

Sauté vegetables in oil until shiny. Add water chestnuts, rice, and shrimp. Simmer for 5 minutes until heated through.

Serves 4.

Broccoli-Rice Casserole

· 1 ½ c. cooked rice
· 1 egg, beaten
· ¾ c. shredded cheddar cheese, divided
· 1 (10 oz.) package frozen chopped broccoli
· 1 Tbsp. minced onion
· ⅓ c. milk
· 2 eggs, beaten
· ¼ tsp. pepper
· 1 (4 oz.) jar sliced mushrooms, drained

Preheat oven to 375°.

Combine rice, 1 egg, and ½ c. cheese, mixing well. Press mixture into a greased 9-inch pie plate; set aside.

Cook broccoli according to package directions; drain well. Add ¼ cup cheese and remaining ingredients to broccoli; mix well. Pour broccoli mixture into rice-lined pie plate. Bake at 375° for about 50 minutes, or until done.

Quinoa Salad

· 4 c. chicken or vegetable broth
· 1 ½ c. raw whole grain quinoa
· 2 cucumbers, sliced
· 1 orange or yellow bell pepper, diced
· ½ bunch parsley, chopped finely
· 4 tomatoes, chopped
· ¼ c. olive oil
· ⅓ c. lemon juice
· 2 cloves garlic, minced
· Salt and pepper, to taste

Cook quinoa in broth until it fluffs up, about 15 minutes.

While quinoa is cooking, whisk together lemon juice, olive oil, garlic cloves, salt, and pepper.

When quinoa is finished cooking, allow to cool slightly, then toss with vegetables and lemon juice mixture stirring well to combine.

Serves 6.

Fiesta Quinoa Pilaf

· 1 tsp. olive oil
· ½ yellow onion, diced
· ½ yellow or orange bell pepper, seeded and diced
· 1 tsp. sea salt
· ¼ tsp. freshly ground black pepper
· 2 cloves garlic, minced
· ½ tsp. ground cumin
· ½ tsp. chili powder
· Pinch of cayenne pepper
· 1 c. red quinoa, rinsed and drained
· Juice of ½ lime
· ¼ c. chopped scallions
· ¼ c. fresh cilantro, chopped, plus more for garnish

Heat olive oil in a medium saucepan over medium-high heat. Add onion, bell pepper, salt, and black pepper, and sauté until soft, about 3 minutes. Stir in garlic, cumin, chili powder, and cayenne, and cook for 1 more minute. Stir in quinoa and broth. Cover, reduce heat, and simmer for 15 to 20 minutes until all liquid is absorbed and quinoa is plumped up. Remove from heat, fluff with a fork, and let sit for five minutes, covered. Stir in lime juice, scallions and cilantro; serve.

French Onion Rice

· ¼ c. butter or margarine
· 1 c. rice
· 1 c. water
· 1 large onion, chopped
· 1 (10 ½ oz.) can Campbell's® French Onion Soup, undiluted
· Parsley flakes or fresh parsley, chopped

Preheat oven to 350°.

Melt butter in oblong casserole dish. Add remaining ingredients, except parsley flakes. Stir to mix. Sprinkle parsley flakes over top. Bake uncovered at 350° for 1 hour.

Serves 8.

Mexican Rice

· ½ c. chopped onion
· 2 tsp. butter or oil
· 2 cloves garlic, chopped (or 2 tsp of jarred minced garlic)
· 1 tsp. cumin seed
· 1 c. white rice (brown rice can be substituted)
· 2 ¾ c. water (3 ¾ if using brown rice)
· 1 ½ cubes Caldo de Sopa Tomate
  (found in Mexican Food aisle)

Sauté onion, then add garlic and rice and brown slightly. Boil water to dissolve cubes of Caldo de Sopa Tomate, and then add to rice. Bring to a boil and simmer with lid on about 20 minutes (more for brown rice) until water is absorbed. Add cracked pepper, if desired.

Risotto

· 1 c. uncooked Arborio rice
· 3 Tbsp. butter or margarine, melted
· ½ small onion, chopped
· ¼ c. dry white wine
· 1 garlic clove, minced
· 3 c. chicken broth, heated
· ¼ tsp. salt
· 2 Tbsp. freshly grated Parmesan cheese

Cook rice in melted butter in a large skillet over high heat one minute, stirring constantly. Reduce heat to medium high and add onion; sauté 1 to 3 minutes until onion is tender. Stir in wine and garlic, cook until wine is absorbed. Add 1 cup warm broth, stirring constantly, until liquid is absorbed. Repeat procedure, adding remaining broth 1 cup at a time, allowing liquid to be absorbed after each addition, stirring constantly. (This will take 30 to 45 minutes).

Remove from heat and add salt and cheese. Stir until blended.

Variations:
Herbed Risotto
Stir in 2 Tbsp. chopped fresh herbs during last 5 minutes of cooking.

Mushroom Risotto
Before beginning risotto, place 3 oz. of fresh portobello mushrooms in a cast iron skillet. Drizzle with 2 Tbsp. olive oil, sprinkle with salt and pepper. Roast at 500° for 4 minutes, turn over and roast 4 minutes more. (Mushrooms may smoke and sizzle.) Chop mushrooms and set aside; stir gently into risotto just before serving.

Low-fat Two-Cheese Polenta

· 1 c. 1% low-fat milk
· 1 c. water
· 1 ¼ tsp. salt
· ¼ tsp. freshly ground black pepper
· 1 ¼ c. instant dry polenta
· ⅓ c. fat-free or low-fat cream cheese
· ⅓ c. grated Parmigiano-Reggiano cheese

Combine the first 4 ingredients in a medium saucepan over medium-high heat. Bring to a boil; gradually add polenta, stirring constantly with a whisk. Cook 2 minutes or until thick, stirring constantly. Remove from heat; stir in cheeses. Serve immediately.

Colleen's Escalloped Apples

· 5 or 6 apples, cored, peeled, and chopped
· ¾ c. sugar
· 3 Tbsp. flour
· ¼ c. melted butter
· Ground cinnamon to taste (optional)

Preheat oven to 350°. Butter a medium casserole dish.

Mix together flour and sugar. Combine flour mixture with chopped apples and pour into buttered dish. Pour melted butter over apples and stir lightly to combine. If desired, sprinkle cinnamon over the top of apples.

Cover with foil and bake for 40 to 50 minutes. Remove foil during last 15 minutes of baking time.

Serves 5-6.

Stuffed Apples Baked in Apple Brandy

· ⅔ c. raisins
· ½ c. apple brandy
· 1 ½ c. ground toasted hazelnuts or walnuts
· ½ c. dark brown sugar
· ½ c. whipping cream
· ½ tsp. cinnamon
· ½ tsp. ground nutmeg
· 10 large baking apples
· ⅔ c. apple brandy
· ⅔ c. apple cider
· 1 c. honey
· ¾ c. whole cranberry or lingonberry sauce
· Watercress, for garnish

Preheat oven to 350º.

Combine raisins and ½ cup brandy in large bowl and let stand 15 minutes.

Stir in ground nuts, sugar, cream, cinnamon and nutmeg. Cut ¼-inch slices from tops of apples; remove cores 1 ½-inch from bottom making a 1-inch hollow. Arrange apples ½-inch apart in shallow baking pan and spoon raisin mixture into centers of apples. Combine remaining ingredients and pour over apples.

Bake apples uncovered, basting frequently with pan juices, until apples are tender, 30 to 45 minutes.

Arrange on serving plate, top with cranberry or lingonberry sauce, and garnish with watercress. Serve with pan juices.

Serves 10.

Broccoli Slaw

Salad
- · 1 head of broccoli, finely chopped or shredded (shredded looks better)
- · 1 red onion, chopped
- · ½ lb. bacon, fried crisp and crumbled
- · 1 c. Craisins® (dried cranberries)

Dressing
- · 1 c. mayonnaise
- · ½ c. sugar
- · 2 Tbsp. red wine vinegar

Combine the ingredients for the dressing in a medium bowl, and whisk to combine thoroughly.

Toss together the ingredients for the salad, except the bacon, and combine with dressing to coat. Mix in the bacon just before serving to maintain crispiness.

Bean Salad

- · 1 can green beans, drained
- · 1 can wax yellow beans, drained
- · 1 can red kidney beans, drained and washed
- · 1 small onion, minced, diced or sliced
- · ¾ cup celery, chopped

Dressing
- · 1 c. sugar
- · ⅓ c. regular vinegar
- · ⅓ c. red wine vinegar
- · 1 tsp. salt
- · 1 tsp. garlic powder
- · ¼ tsp. pepper
- · ¼ tsp. celery seed
- · ⅛ tsp. dill
- · ⅛ tsp. basil

Combine beans, onions, and celery in bowl. Combine dressing ingredients in a saucepan and bring to boiling point (enough to dissolve sugar). Pour hot mixture over beans in bowl.

Cover tightly and marinate overnight.

Serves 6.

Desserts

White Chocolate Cake

Cake
· ¼ lb. white chocolate (or almond bark)
· 1 ½ c. water
· 4 eggs, separated
· 1 c. butter
· 2 c. sugar
· 1 tsp. vanilla
· 2 ½ c. flour, sifted
· 1 ½ tsp. salt
· 1 tsp. baking soda
· 1 c. buttermilk
· 1 (3 ½ oz.) package instant vanilla pudding

Icing
· 1 (8 oz.) package cream cheese
· ½ c. butter
· 1 box confectioner's sugar
· 1 tsp. vanilla
· Coconut (optional)

For Cake: Preheat oven to 350°. Grease, flour, and line with wax paper three 9-inch layer pans.

Melt white chocolate in 1 ½ cups boiling water; cool. Beat egg whites until stiff; set aside. Cream together butter and sugar until fluffy. Add egg yolks one at a time and beat well after each addition. Add melted chocolate and vanilla; mix well.

Sift dry ingredients together and add alternately with buttermilk to the creamed mixture. Beat after each addition until smooth.

Fold in stiffly beaten egg whites. Pour equally into the three cake pans. Bake 30 to 35 minutes. Remove to cooling racks to cool. Make pudding according to package directions; chill.

For Icing: Mix together cream cheese and butter. Add confectioner's sugar and vanilla; mix until creamy. Set in refrigerator to chill until spreading consistency. Spread pudding between layers of cake. Frost top and sides of cake with chilled icing. Press coconut into icing. Keep cake refrigerated.

Serves 16.

7-Up® Pound Cake

· 2 sticks margarine or butter
· 1 ½ c. oil
· 3 c. sugar
· 5 eggs
· 3 c. flour
· 1 c. 7-Up® (not diet)
· 1 tsp. lemon extract
· ½ tsp. almond extract

Preheat oven to 350°.

Cream margarine or butter, oil, and sugar. Add eggs, one at a time. Mix in flour, alternating with 7-Up® and flavorings. Bake in a greased and floured tube or Bundt cake pan for 1 hour 15 minutes or until cake tests done by inserting a toothpick.

Serves 16 - 20.

Arta's Black and White Cake

Cake
· 1 box brown sugar (16 oz.)
· I stick butter
· 3 eggs at room temperature
· 1 square unsweetened chocolate, melted
· 2 ½ c. sifted cake flour
· ¾ c. buttermilk
· ¾ c. ice water
· 1 tsp. baking soda (stir into ice water)
· 1 tsp. vanilla

Chocolate Icing
· ¾ stick butter
· ½ square unsweetened chocolate, melted
· 1 (1 lb.) box confectioner's sugar
· Cream or milk
· 1 tsp. vanilla
· Few drops almond flavor
· 1 ½ c. pecans

White Icing
· 1 egg white
· ½ c. sugar
· 1 Tbsp. ice water
· ¼ tsp. cream of tartar
· Pinch of salt
· ¼ tsp. vanilla (optional)

For cake: Grease and flour 9×13-inch pan. Cream together brown sugar, butter, and eggs; add melted chocolate. Mix in flour alternately with liquid ingredients. Put in COLD oven; set oven to 350°. Bake 35 to 45 minutes until cake pulls away from edge and bubbles in middle.

Mix together ingredients for chocolate icing, using enough cream or milk to reach spreading consistency. Spread on warm cake.

Combine ingredients for white icing in bowl placed over pan of boiling water (off stove). Beat until it peaks. Spread over half of the chocolate icing or double the ingredients and cover entire cake.

Serves 12.

Nonna's Chocolate Cake

In a bowl combine:
· 2 c. flour, sifted
· 2 c. sugar
· ½ tsp. salt
· 1 tsp. soda

Preheat oven to 425°.

In a saucepan combine:
· 1 ¼ c. shortening
· 1 c. water
· ½ c. butter
· 4 Tbsp. cocoa

Heat to boiling and then combine with
the above dry ingredients.

Add:
· ½ c. buttermilk
· 2 eggs
· 1 Tbsp. vanilla

Beat well and pour into greased and floured
9×13×2-inch pan. Bake at 425° for 25 minutes.
The middle of the cake will split as it bakes.

Icing
· 4 Tbsp. cocoa
· 4 Tbsp. milk
· 1 tsp. vanilla
· ½ c. butter
· Dash of salt
· ⅔ box of powdered sugar

Bring cocoa and butter to a boil. Add milk, salt, vanilla, and
powdered sugar. Mix well until smooth and have ready
when cake comes out. Ice while hot.

Photo provided by Nonna's

Blueberry Sour Cream Pound Cake

· ½ lb. butter
· 3 c. sugar
· 6 eggs
· 3 c. (heaping) flour
· 1 ¼ tsp. baking soda
· ¾ c. sour cream
· ½ tsp. vanilla
· ½ c. milk
· 1 can blueberries, well drained

Let all ingredients reach room temperature.
Preheat oven to 325 °. Grease and flour 3 loaf pans or 1
tube pan.

Cream butter and sugar. Add eggs one at a time, beating
well after each. Sift flour with soda. Add 2 C. of the flour
and mix alternately with sour cream. Add vanilla, remaining
flour mix, and milk. Fold in drained blueberries. Pour batter
into prepared pans. Loaf pans: bake for 1 hour. Tube pan:
bake for 1 hour and 20 minutes.

Serves 20 - 30.

Italian Cream Cake

Cake
· 1 c. buttermilk
· 1 tsp. baking soda
· 5 eggs, separated
· 2 c. sugar
· ½ c. margarine or butter
· 1 ½ c. shortening
· 2 c. sifted flour
· 1 tsp. vanilla
· 1 c. chopped pecans
· 1 ⅓ c. shredded coconut

Icing
· 1 (8 oz.) package cream cheese, softened
· ½ c. margarine or butter
· 1 (1 lb.) box confectioner's sugar
· 1 tsp. vanilla
· 1 c. chopped pecans

For the cake: Preheat oven to 325°. Grease and flour three
9-inch layer pans.

Combine soda and buttermilk; let stand a few minutes.
Beat egg whites until stiff. Cream sugar, butter or
margarine, and shortening. Add egg yolks, one at time,
beating well after each. Add buttermilk mixture alternately
with flour to creamed mixture. Stir in vanilla, pecans, and
coconut. Fold in egg whites. Pour batter equally into
prepared pans. Bake 25 minutes or until cake tests done.

Cool in pans 10 minutes; remove to cooling racks.

For the icing: Mix cream cheese and margarine or butter
well. Add vanilla. Beat in sugar a little at a time until of
spreading consistency. Spread between layers and on
top and sides of cooled cake. Sprinkle top with chopped
pecans.

Serves 10 - 12.

Variation: Fold 1 ½ cup chopped maraschino cherries into
cake batter. Can also make 12×17-inch sheet cake.

J.C. Watts' Oklahoma Mud Cake

Cake
· 1 ½ c. sugar
· 2 sticks butter or margarine
· 2 Tbsp. cocoa
· 4 eggs
· 1 Tbsp. vanilla
· 1 ½ c. flour
· 1 ½ c. coconut
· 1 ½ c. chopped nuts

Preheat oven to 350°.

Cream together sugar, butter, cocoa, vanilla, and eggs. Mix well. Mix in remaining ingredients. Pour into a 9×13-inch pan. Bake at 350° for 45 minutes, or until done.

Oklahoma Mud Frosting
· 1 jar marshmallow cream
· 1 box powdered sugar
· 1 stick butter or margarine
· 1 Tbsp. vanilla
· 1 ½ c. milk

After cake is done and still hot, spread one jar of marshmallow cream on top of cake. Allow cake to cool completely. Then mix powdered sugar, butter, vanilla, and milk. Cream together and spread over cake.

Mayor's Old Fashion Chocolate Sheet Cake

Cake
· 2 c. flour
· 2 c. granulated sugar
· ½ tsp. salt
· ½ lb. butter
· 1 c. water
· 4 Tbsp. cocoa
· 1 tsp. baking soda
· 2 eggs beaten
· 1 tsp. pure vanilla extract
· ½ c. sour cream

Preheat oven to 350°.

Mix flour, sugar, and salt in a mixing bowl and set aside. In a medium saucepan, melt the butter. Add water and cocoa, mix well, and bring to a boil. Add to the flour and mix. Add remaining ingredients, stir and pour into 11×17-inch pan. Bake at 350 ° for 20 minutes.

Icing
· 8 Tbsp. butter
· 6 Tbsp. cocoa
· 6 Tbsp. milk
· 1 lb. sugar
· 1 tsp. pure vanilla extract
· 1 c. pecans

In a medium saucepan, melt butter. Add cocoa and milk. Bring to a boil; remove from heat. Add sugar, vanilla, and nuts. Mix well, cool slightly, and pour over cake.

Gooey Butter Cake

Bottom layer
· 1 (3 oz.) package cream cheese, softened
· 1 box yellow cake mix
· 1 egg
· 1 Tbsp. cold water
· ½ c. butter or margarine

Top layer
· 1 (1 lb.) box confectioner's sugar
· 1 (8 oz.) package cream cheese, softened
· 1 tsp. vanilla
· 2 eggs

Preheat oven to 350°.

Grease and flour a 9x13-inch pan.

Mix the 3 oz. package cream cheese with the cake mix, 1 egg, cold water, and butter. Batter will be slightly stiff. Spread in prepared pan; set aside.

Mix confectioner's sugar, 8 oz. cream cheese, vanilla, and eggs. Spread over first batter already in the pan.

Bake 40 minutes.

Dust with powdered sugar and let cool in pan.

Serves 12.

Old-Fashioned Pound Cake

· 1 ⅔ c. sugar
· 1 c. shortening
· 5 eggs
· 1 tsp. lemon juice
· ½ tsp. vanilla
· ½ tsp. almond extract
· 2 c. well-sifted flour

Preheat oven to 350°. Grease and flour a tube or Bundt cake pan.

Cream well the sugar and shortening. Add eggs one at a time beating well after each addition. Add lemon juice and flavorings. Add flour gradually. Beat well and pour into prepared pan.

Bake 55 to 60 minutes.

Serves 12 - 15.

Waldorf Red Cake

Cake
· ½ c. shortening
· 1 ½ c. sugar
· 2 eggs
· 2 tsp. cocoa
· 2 oz. red food coloring
· 1 c. buttermilk
· 2 ¼ c. cake flour
· 1 tsp. salt
· 1 tsp. vanilla
· 1 Tbsp. vinegar
· 1 tsp. baking soda

Preheat oven to 350°. Grease and flour 2 layer cake pans.

Cream shortening, sugar, and eggs until light and fluffy. Mix cocoa and food coloring. Add to creamed mixture. Add buttermilk alternately with sifted flour and salt. Stir in vanilla. Add soda to vinegar and blend in (do not beat). Pour batter into prepared pans.

Bake 30 to 35 minutes. Cool in pans for 10 minutes. Remove to cooling racks. When completely cool, frost between layers, sides, and top of cake.

Frosting
· 3 Tbsp. flour
· 1 c. milk
· 1 c. sugar
· 1 c. butter or margarine
· 1 tsp. vanilla

Cook flour and milk over medium heat until thick, stirring constantly using wire whisk. Cover and cool. Cream butter and sugar until mixture is very light and fluffy and add vanilla. Stir milk mixture into creamed ingredients and blend well. Do not overbeat. Frosting should be like whipped cream.

Serves 16.

Oatmeal Cake

For the Cake
· 1 c. quick oats
· 1 stick margarine
· 1 ¼ c. boiling water
· 1 ⅓ c. flour
· ¼ tsp. salt
· 1 tsp. cinnamon
· 1 tsp. nutmeg
· 1 tsp. baking soda
· 1 c. sugar
· 1 c. brown sugar
· 2 eggs

For the Topping
· 1 ½ sticks margarine
· 2 c. brown sugar
· ½ c. milk
· 2 ½ c. coconut
· 1 c. pecans

Preheat oven to 350°. Grease a 9×13-baking pan.

Stir together first three ingredients and set aside. Mix together flour, salt, cinnamon, nutmeg, baking soda, sugar, brown sugar, and eggs. Add to oatmeal mixture and mix well. Pour into prepared pan and bake 35 minutes.

Increase heat to 500°.

Mix together topping ingredients and spread on warm cake. Bake at 500° until bubbly (less than 5 minutes).

Baked Fudge

Preheat oven to 300°.

Mix
· 2 c. sugar
· 1 ½ c. flour
· ½ c. cocoa

Add
· 4 well-beaten eggs
· 1 c. melted margarine
· 2 tsp. vanilla
· 1 c. chopped pecans (optional)
· Whipped cream

Bake in a 9×9-inch pan sitting in a larger pan of hot water at 300° for at least 1 hour. Test by inserting knife. Fudge should be firm like custard, but not stiff like brownies.

Top with whipped cream.

Peanut Butter Fudge

· 2 c. sugar
· ⅔ c. milk
· 1 c. peanut butter
· 1 (7 oz.) jar marshmallow cream
· 1 tsp. vanilla (optional)

Cook sugar and milk to soft ball stage, 236° on a candy thermometer. Remove from heat and add remaining ingredients. Mix thoroughly and pour into 8×8-inch buttered pan.

Serves 16.

Note – This recipe does not double well.

Sherri Coale's Chocolate Chip Cheese Ball

· 8 oz. cream cheese, softened
· ¼ tsp. vanilla
· 2 Tbsp. brown sugar
· ¾ c. finely chopped pecans
· ½ c. butter (no substitutes), softened
· ¾ c. powdered sugar
· ¾ c. miniature semi-sweet chocolate chips
· Graham crackers

Beat the cream cheese, butter, and vanilla until fluffy. Gradually add sugar; beat until combined. Stir in chocolate chips. Cover and chill for 2 hours.

Put cream cheese mixture on a large piece of plastic wrap; shape into a ball and chill another hour. Before serving, roll cheese ball in pecans.

Serve with graham crackers.

Amaretto Cheesecake

Crust
· ¾ c. graham cracker crumbs
· ¾ c. amaretto crumbs (from amaretto biscuits)
· ¼ c. sugar
· 4 Tbsp. softened butter

Filling
· 1 lb. cottage cheese
· 1 lb. cream cheese
· 1 ½ c. sugar
· 4 eggs
· 3 Tbsp. cornstarch
· 3 Tbsp. flour
· 1 tsp. vanilla extract
· 1 tsp. almond extract
· ¼ c. amaretto liqueur
· 1 ¼ c. amaretto biscuit crumbs
· 1 ½ c. sour cream
· ½ c. melted butter

Preheat oven to 350°.

Crust: Add butter and sugar to crumbs in processor bowl and process for 5 seconds to a fine texture. Pat into buttered 9-inch spring form pan. Bake for 6 minutes and cool.

Filling: Place all cheeses in food processor container with steel blade and blend until smooth. With motor running, gradually add the sugar through the tube. Add eggs, cornstarch, flour, vanilla extract, almond extract, and amaretto liqueur. Blend until smooth. Place in large bowl and beat in amaretto crumbs, sour cream, and melted butter. Pour into prepared spring form pan and bake for 1 hour, 20 minutes. Turn off oven and let cool in oven for 3 hours. Chill overnight in pan wrapped in foil. Remove spring form.

Serves 20.

Cedric Jones' New York Giants Cheesecake

· 2 c. graham cracker crumbs
· 2 ½ Tbsp. sugar
· 1 tsp. ground cinnamon
· 1 ¼ tsp. ground nutmeg
· ½ c. butter, melted
· 3 (8 oz.) packages cream cheese, softened
· 1 c. sugar
· 2 Tbsp. all-purpose flour
· ⅛ tsp. salt
· 5 eggs, separated and at room temperature
· 1 egg
· 1 ½ c. sour cream
· ¼ c. sugar

Preheat oven to 300°.

Combine first five ingredients; mixing well. Press firmly into a 9-inch spring form pan; chill. Beat cream cheese with electric mixer on low speed until light and fluffy; gradually add 1 C. sugar, mixing well. Stir in flour and salt. Add 5 egg yolks and 1 whole egg, one at a time, beating well after each addition. Stir in the sour cream. Beat egg whites until foamy. Gradually add ¼ C. sugar, 1 Tbsp. at a time, beating until stiff peaks form. Fold into the cream cheese mixture; pour into prepared pan. Bake at 300° for 90 minutes. Turn off oven and allow the cheesecake to cool in the oven for 3 hours. Chill for 4 to 6 hours or overnight.

Serve plain or with your favorite topping.

Serves 12.

Cheesecake Cupcakes

· 24 vanilla wafers
· ¾ c. sugar
· 2 (8 oz.) packages cream cheese, softened
· 2 tsp. lemon juice
· 2 eggs
· 1 tsp. vanilla
· 1 (1 lb. 5 oz.) can cherry pie filling

Preheat oven to 350°.

Line 24 muffin tins (1 ½-inch size) with paper liners. Place 1 vanilla wafer in bottom of each tin.

Blend sugar, cream cheese, lemon juice, eggs, and vanilla in bowl. Fill tins halfway with mixture. Bake for 20 minutes at 350°. Cool.

Top with pie filling. Keep refrigerated.

Serves 24.

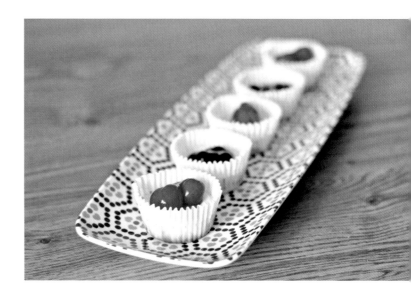

Blueberry Amaretto Squares

· 1 ¾ c. graham cracker crumbs
· 1 ½ c. sugar
· ½ c. margarine, melted
· 2 eggs
· ¾ c. sugar
· 1 (8 oz.) package cream cheese, softened
· 2 ½ c. milk
· 2 (3 ¾ oz.) packages instant vanilla pudding
· ½ c. amaretto, divided
· 1 ¼ c. sugar
· ¼ c. cornstarch
· 5 c. frozen blueberries, thawed
· 1 (8 oz.) carton frozen whipped topping, thawed

Preheat oven to 350°.

Combine first three ingredients; press into greased 9×13×2-inch baking dish. Combine eggs, ¾ cup sugar, and cream cheese; beat with electric mixer until smooth. Spread mixture over graham cracker crumbs. Bake for 30 minutes at 350°; then cool completely.

Combine milk, pudding mix, and ¼ cup amaretto; beat 2 minutes at a low speed with mixer. Spread over cream cheese layer.

Combine 1 ¼ cup sugar and cornstarch in large saucepan. Gradually add ¼ cup amaretto; stirring until smooth. Stir in blueberries. Cook over medium heat, stirring constantly, until thickened. Cool. Pour blueberry mixture over pudding mixture. Chill thoroughly.

Before serving, spread whipped topping over blueberries.

Dandy Apricot Squares

· ½ c. cooked apricots, drained
· 1½ c. granulated sugar, divided
· ⅓ c. water
· 2 c. sifted flour
· ½ tsp. salt
· ½ tsp. baking soda
· ¾ c. butter or margarine
· 1 c. chopped pecans

Preheat oven to 400°.

Combine cooked apricots, ¾ cup granulated sugar, and water; cook about 5 minutes, stirring occasionally, until slightly thickened. Cool.

Sift flour, salt, and soda together. Cream butter, gradually adding ¾ cup granulated sugar; beat well. Blend in dry ingredients. Stir in pecans. Press 3 cups of this crumbly mixture in bottom and half-way up sides of greased 9×13×2-inch pan. Bake at 400° for 10 minutes.

Spread apricot mixture over crust and sprinkle rest of crumbs over top. Bake 20 to 25 minutes. Cool. Cut in squares.

Top with whipped cream if desired.

Serves 12.

Chocolate and Oatmeal Cookies

Preheat oven to 400°.

Cream together:
· 2 c. butter
· 2 c. sugar
· 2 c. brown sugar

Add:
· 4 eggs
· 2 tsp. vanilla

In a separate bowl mix together:
· 4 c. flour
· 5 c. oatmeal (Measure out 5 c. of oatmeal only and
    powder in small amounts using blender)
· 1 tsp. salt
· 2 tsp. baking powder
· 2 tsp. baking soda

Mix all ingredients together.

Add:
· 1 (24 oz.) bag of chocolate chips
· 1 (8 oz.) plain Hershey bar, finely grated

Bake at 400° on ungreased cookie sheet 2 inches apart for 6 to 8 minutes.

Italian Anise Cookies

Cookies
· ½ c. butter, softened
· ½ c. sugar
· 3 large eggs
· 2 tsp. anise extract (or almond extract)
· 2 ½ c. all-purpose flour (may need up to 3 c.)
· 1 Tbsp. baking powder
· 2 - 3 Tbsp. milk

Icing
· 2 c. confectioners' sugar
· 3 Tbsp. milk
· ⅛ tsp. anise extract
· Food coloring (optional)
· Decorative candy sprinkles (optional)

Preheat oven to 350°. Line cookie sheets with parchment paper.

For cookies: cream the butter and sugar until light and fluffy, about 5 minutes. Add eggs, one at a time, mixing after each addition. Add anise extract.

Blend flour and baking powder. Start by adding ⅓ dry ingredients to the butter/sugar in your mixer, then add 1 Tbsp. milk. Add another ⅓ of the flour and another 1 Tbsp. milk. Finally, mix in enough of the remaining flour until your dough is like a brownie batter (it should be softer than a drop cookie dough). Use a cookie scooper to make simple round drop cookies – use wet fingers to pat any rough edges OR for an Easter-Egg look, roll 1 Tbsp. dough into an elongated ball. Bake cookies 10 to 12 minutes (they won't be brown, but the insides will be soft and cake-like).

For icing: Mix sugar, milk, and extract to make a sugar glaze. Add food coloring if desired. Hold cookie and turn upside down to dip the top half in the glaze; turn over and immediately top with sprinkles so they will stick. Allow icing to harden overnight; store in air-tight containers or freeze.

Vanilla-Champagne Soaked Fruit

· 1 bottle champagne
· ¾ c. sugar
· 1 vanilla bean, split
· 3 Tbsp. fresh mint, chopped
· 1 cantaloupe, halved
· 1 pt. fresh raspberries
· 1 large orange, peeled and sectioned
· ½ honeydew melon, peeled and chopped

Bring the first 3 ingredients to a boil in a saucepan over high heat. Stir until sugar is dissolved (about 5 minutes). Reduce heat to medium and cook until mixture is reduced by half (about 10 minutes). Remove from heat and stir in mint. Let stand 5 minutes then pour mixture into a strainer. Scrape vanilla seeds into bowl and stir.

Cut cantaloupe into thin wedges and place into a baking dish. Add raspberries, orange, and melon. Pour warm syrup over fruit. Cover and chill 3 hours.

Remove fruit from syrup using slotted spoon and arrange on a serving platter.

Serves 4-6.

Raspberry Torte

· 1 c. flour
· ½ c. confectioner's sugar
· ½ c. butter, softened
· 1 (10 oz.) package raspberries, thawed
· ¾ c. chopped walnuts
· 2 eggs
· 1 c. sugar
· ¼ c. all-purpose flour
· ½ tsp. baking powder
· ½ tsp. salt
· 1 tsp. vanilla

Raspberry Sauce

· ½ c. sugar
· 2 Tbsp. cornstarch
· ½ c. water
· 1 Tbsp. lemon juice
· Reserved raspberry juice

Preheat oven to 350°.

For sauce: In small saucepan combine all ingredients except lemon juice. Cook, stirring constantly until clear. Add lemon juice.

For torte: In small mixing bowl, combine 1 cup flour, confectioner's sugar, and butter. Blend well. Press into bottom of 9-inch, ungreased, square pan. Bake 15 minutes in 350° oven. Cool.

Drain raspberries, reserving liquid for sauce. Spread berries over crust; sprinkle with walnuts.

In small bowl, mix eggs, sugar, ¼ cup flour, salt, baking powder, and vanilla at low speed. Blend well. Pour over walnuts and crust. Bake at 350° for 35 to 40 minutes until golden brown. Cool.

Cut in squares and serve with whipped cream and raspberry sauce.

Serves 8 - 10.

Legend's Autumn Nut Torte

Cake
· 6 eggs
· 1 ½ c. sugar
· 3 Tbsp. all-purpose flour
· 5 tsp. orange juice
· ¾ tsp. baking powder
· ¼ tsp. salt
· 1 ¼ lbs. pecans, finely grated
· 1 c. whipping cream
· Minced zest of 1 small orange

Icing
· 9 oz. semi-sweet chocolate
· 2 egg yolks
· ¾ c. confectioner's sugar
· ¾ c. sour cream

For cake: Preheat oven to 350°. Cut waxed paper to line bottoms of 3 (4 ½×8 ½-inch) baking pans.

Separate eggs. Beat whites until stiff, but not dry; set aside. Combine yolks with next five ingredients in large bowl and beat until fluffy. Fold pecans into yolk mixture. Stir in about ¼ whites to loosen batter. Gently fold in remaining whites. Divide among baking pans and bake until cake pulls away from sides of pans (center of cakes will still be moist), about 25 minutes. Let cool.

Whip cream until stiff. Beat in orange zest. Slice each cake horizontally to form 2 layers. Frost with cream between each layer, stacking to make 6 layers. Refrigerate torte.

For icing: Melt chocolate in double boiler. Combine egg yolks, sugar, and sour cream in small bowl and beat until smooth. Add to melted chocolate, whisking constantly, and cook about 2 minutes. Frost cold torte while icing is still warm.

Serves 12 - 14.

*Comment: Appeared in Bon Appetit magazine and the Best of Bon Appetit cookbook.

The Very Best Chocolate Pie Filling

· 3 c. milk
· 3 oz. unsweetened chocolate (3 squares)
· 1 c. sugar
· 4 Tbsp. cornstarch
· 2 Tbsp. flour
· ¼ tsp. salt
· 2 egg yolks, slightly beaten
· 2 tsp. vanilla

Scald 1 cup of the milk with the chocolate, stirring until thick and smooth. Add 2 cup of milk.

Combine in a bowl in the order given, 1 cup sugar, 4 Tbsp. cornstarch, 2 Tbsp. flour, ¼ tsp. salt.

Remove milk mixture from heat and add dry ingredients, stirring briskly. Return to heat and cook until thick and smooth, stirring constantly. Add a small amount of pudding mixture to slightly beaten egg yolks, then stir yolks into filling. Cook 1 full minute after bubbling starts. Season with vanilla. Cool. Beat before turning into baked pie shell.

Top with meringue or whipped cream.

Serves 8.

Dara Marie's Coconut Cream Pie

· 1 ½ c. sugar
· ½ c. plus 4 tsp. cornstarch
· ¼ tsp. salt
· 6 egg yolks, beaten
· 6 c. milk
· 3 Tbsp. butter
· 1 Tbsp. vanilla
· 2 c. coconut
· 2 prepared pie crusts

Combine milk, egg yolks, cornstarch, sugar, and salt. Cook until thick and smooth while stirring constantly. Let boil 3 to 5 minutes, while continuing to stir. Add butter, vanilla, and coconut. Pour batter while still warm into pie crusts.

Chill in refrigerator for 2 to 3 hours before serving.

Add whipped cream or meringue as desired.

Four Layer Delight

Preheat oven to 350°.

First layer
· 1 c. flour
· ½ c. pecans, chopped
· 1 stick margarine
· ¼ c. sugar

Combine all and press in 9×13-inch pan.
Bake 15 to 20 minutes at 350°. Cool.

Second layer
· 8 oz. cream cheese
· 1 c. confectioner's sugar
· 1 c. prepared whipped topping

Beat cream cheese, add sugar, fold in whipped topping, and spread over crust.

Third layer
· 2 small packages instant butterscotch pudding
· 3 c. milk

Prepare pudding with milk according to package directions. Pour on top of cream cheese layer.

Fourth layer
Top with prepared whipped topping.

Serves 8 - 10.

Fresh Strawberry Pie

· 1 qt. fresh strawberries
· ¾ c. water
· 3 Tbsp. cornstarch
· 1 c. sugar
· 1 tsp. lemon juice
· 1 c. cream, whipped
· 1 9-inch pastry shell

Line a baked pastry shell with fresh strawberries. Reserve 1 C. of the berries for glaze.

Glaze
Simmer 1 C. of berries and ¾ C. water for 3 to 4 minutes. Combine corn starch and sugar. Add to berries along with lemon juice. Cook mixture until thickened and clear. Pour over berries in shell and chill in the refrigerator.

Top with whipped cream.

Lemonade Pie

· 1 graham cracker crust
· 4 ½ oz. Cool Whip®
· 1 (14 oz.) can sweetened condensed milk
· 1 (6 oz.) can frozen lemonade, thawed
· Whipped cream (optional)
· Lemon rind (optional)

Combine Cool Whip®, sweetened condensed milk, and lemonade. Spoon mixture into graham cracker pie shell and freeze (covered).

Garnish with whipped cream or a lemon rind if desired.

No Fail Pie Crust

· ½ c. shortening
· 3 Tbsp. water
· 1 ½ c. flour, sifted
· 1 tsp. sugar
· ⅛ tsp. salt
· Nonstick cooking spray

Preheat oven to 375°.

Mix together shortening, sugar, flour, and salt with a fork until it resembles cornmeal. Add 3 Tbsp. of water, 1 Tbsp. at a time, until dough sticks together.

Spray a 9-inch pie pan with nonstick cooking spray and add the pie crust to the pie pan. Press the batter into the pan starting at the edges. Prick bottom with a fork and bake at 375° for about 25 minutes or until it turns golden brown.

Pecan Pie

· ½ c. butter or margarine
· 1 c. sugar
· 1 c. light corn syrup
· 4 eggs, beaten
· 1 tsp. vanilla
· ¼ tsp. salt
· 1 c. pecans
· 1 9-inch unbaked pie shell

Preheat oven to 325°.

Combine butter, sugar, and corn syrup. Cook over low heat, stirring constantly until sugar is dissolved. Cool.

Combine eggs, vanilla, and salt; mix well. Slowly add to cooled butter and sugar mixture; mix well.

Pour filling into pie shell and top with pecans.

Bake at 325° for 50 to 55 minutes.

Pineapple Cream Pie

· 2 graham cracker crusts
· 1 large box instant vanilla pudding
· 1 ½ c. milk
· 1 large can crushed pineapple, drained
· 16 oz. low-fat sour cream
· 1 c. Cool Whip®

Mix pudding with milk and pour into bowl with crushed pineapple. Stir in sour cream and Cool Whip®. Pour over graham cracker crusts.

Refrigerate overnight or freeze.

Steve Owens' Favorite Apple Pie

Double-crust recipe
· 2 c. sifted all-purpose flour
· ½ tsp. salt
· ⅔ c. shortening
· 5 - 6 Tbsp. cold water

Apple pie
· 6 c. apples, peeled and sliced
· 1 c. sugar
· ½ tsp. cinnamon
· ¼ tsp. salt
· 2 Tbsp. flour
· 2 Tbsp. butter or margarine
· 1 ½ tsp. lemon juice

Preheat oven to 375°.

For crust: Combine ingredients for crust together and roll out 2 large circles larger than pie pan.

For pie: Arrange apples in layers on bottom crust. Sprinkle mixture of cinnamon, sugar, salt, and flour over apples. Dot with butter or margarine. Pour lemon juice over filling. Place top crust over filling. Seal the top and bottom crust together.

Bake at 375° for 50 minutes. (Until apple slices are tender). Serve with French vanilla ice cream.

Chocolate Sauce

· 1 stick unsalted butter
· 1 c. sugar
· ⅓ c. cocoa
· 1 c. heavy cream
· ⅛ tsp. salt
· 1 tsp. instant freeze-dried coffee, dry
· 1 tsp. vanilla

Melt butter in medium saucepan over low heat. Add sugar, cocoa, cream, and salt. Stir over medium heat until boiling. Add coffee and stir until it dissolves. Reduce heat and simmer, uncovered, 5 minutes. Remove from heat and add vanilla.

Serve hot, warm, or at room temperature.

(Yields 2 ½ Cups)

Grand Marnier® Sauce

· 5 egg yolks (room temperature)
· ¾ c. plus 1 Tbsp. sugar
· ¼ c. Grand Marnier®
· 1 c. heavy cream
· Fresh, seasonal berries of your choice

In top of double boiler, beat egg yolks with a whisk until light yellow in color. Whisk in the ¾ cup sugar and place over simmering water. Continue to whisk and cook until thick, about 20 minutes. Remove from heat and whisk until cooled. Stir in Grand Marnier®. With an electric mixer on medium speed, beat the heavy cream in a bowl until thickened, but still pourable. Add the 1 Tbsp. sugar and stir to mix. Fold into the Grand Marnier® mixture, cover, and refrigerate at least 8 hours or overnight.

Serve Grand Marnier® sauce over fresh berries for a light, elegant dessert.

Praline Sauce

· 1 c. dark corn syrup
· ¼ c. cornstarch
· 2 Tbsp. brown sugar
· 1 tsp. vanilla
· 1 ½ c. chopped pecans, toasted slightly

Combine corn syrup, cornstarch, and brown sugar in a small saucepan. Cook and stir until thickened and bubbly. Remove from heat; stir in vanilla. Cool slightly. Before serving, stir in pecans.

Serve over vanilla ice cream.

(Yields 1 ½ Cups)

Mexican Flan

· 8 eggs
· ⅔ c. sugar
· ¼ tsp. salt
· 3 ½ c. evaporated milk
· 2 tsp. vanilla
· ½ c. brown sugar, firmly packed

Preheat oven to 350°.

Beat eggs until well blended. Add white sugar and salt; mix well. Beat in milk and add vanilla.

Sift the brown sugar into the bottom of a loaf pan. Pour custard gently over sugar. Place loaf pan in a shallow baking pan containing hot (not boiling) water.

Bake at 350° for 1 hour or until knife inserted in center comes out clean. Refrigerate overnight.

Serves 8.

Our Sponsors

Sooners
($500 & above)

OU Physicians

WOMEN'S HEALTH
CENTER

Appointment Access Center
405-271-2222

Anne & Bill McCurdy

Northstar Properties of Oklahoma City, LLC
Savannah Square
Savannah Harbor
The Port at the Trails
Alameda Pointe
Savannah Ridge

Visionary
($250-$499)

Aaron & Jolene Curry
Astellas Pharma Technologies, Inc.
Dirk & Stephanie O' Hara
Insurance Solutions by Irwin Agency Inc.
Le Visage Day Spa
Patriot Ford, Sam & Lori Wampler

X-celerator
($100-$249)

Havenbrook Funeral Home
Paul, Katie, Ashley, & Austin Ihrig
Raising Cane's Chicken Fingers in Norman
Stephanie Powers
Shannon & David Tan

Circle of Friends
($25-$99)

Ashley Streight, Esq.
C. C. & Inez Adams
Carolina Cunningham
Crystal Robinson
Dean & Kristie McKinney
Diane Dragg
Elliott & Meghan Mullinax
Erin Hofmann
Erin Cowan
Imants, Becca, & Brantley Vermelis
Jake, Sarah, & Sebastian Smith
Mike, Kym, & Brady Johnston
Michael Clardy / Clardy Sound
Monty, Liz, Corbin, & Finley Johnson
Nell Pryor
Pam Salamy
Rick & Sharon Rentzel
Rooney Virgin
Shirley Robinson
Taylor & Colton McKinney
Vermelis Custom Cabinets, LLC

Recipe Index

Subject Index

Beverages

Bread

Breakfast

Broccoli

Cabbage

Cake

Lamb

Lighter Fare

Marinades & Rubs

Mexican